THE PUBLIC SPEAKER'S BIBLE

Distributed by
STERLING PUBLISHING CO., INC.
387 Park Avenue South
New York, N. Y. 10016-8810

D1293105

THE PUBLIC SPEAKER'S BIBLE

The definitive guide to speaking in public

by

Stuart Turner

THORSONS PUBLISHING GROUP

First published 1988

© Stuart Turner 1988

British Library Cataloguing in Publication Data

Turner, Stuart
The public speaker's bible.
1. Public speaking
I. Title
808.5'1

ISBN 0 7225 1474 3

*Published by Thorsons Publishing Group,
Wellingborough, Northamptonshire,
NN8 2RQ, England*

Printed in Great Britain by Biddles Limited, Guildford, Surrey

3 5 7 9 10 8 6 4 2

Contents

Introduction

We live in a world where the ability to communicate becomes more and more important and one of the most effective ways of communicating, whether to motivate, inform or simply entertain, is by public speaking. Many people have opportunities to communicate in this way yet hesitate to do so because of inexperience or, most likely, nerves. This is a pity because nerves can be contained with the right approach and, by making an effort, it is possible for almost anyone to make a competent speech.

This book covers the whole field from small social occasions to major business presentations, but the basic essentials of audience analysis and careful preparation apply to all situations and are covered in Part I. The second part of the book is a collection of quotations and anecdotes which you may consider building into your speech to lighten it. But caution: *don't* just dip into Part II and sprinkle your speech with extracts but instead read Part I first so that you understand the wider aspects of the art.

Two final points:

- For 'he' read 'she' throughout.

- The material in Part II has been collected from many sources over the years—if I have inadvertently broken any copyright I would be happy to correct this in future editions.

Stuart Turner

PART I

1

The audience

There won't be too many firm 'rules' laid down in this book because public speaking is an art not a science, but I must start with one: *keep your audience in mind at all times*. A speech must be 'user-friendly' and its success will largely depend on how well you have tailored it to your audience. And remember: the message which is taken away is not what you have said, but what people have *understood* you to have said (which may not be the same thing) so, please, do try to think of things from the point of view of your audience. The absurdity of delivering a robust 'stag' speech to a ladies' luncheon club is obvious but on practically *every* occasion the fine tuning, which comes from really knowing whom you are addressing, will add strength to your words.

So, when you get an invitation to speak, don't rush to accept it. Find out more about the occasion first. Who are the organizers? Are you in sympathy with them and their aims? This will alert you to whether you will be supporting their cause or arguing against it—which might lead to a much rougher ride for you.

Is it an important audience for you or your message? And why have you been asked? Is it because of your natural charm, or because they think you will have something worthwhile to say, or because someone in the inviting organization has heard you speak before? Or are they simply scraping the barrel?

Weigh up all these things before you agree to speak. In some circumstances, of course, you won't receive 'an invitation' as such because you may be the chairman of an association and have little or no choice about speaking, but even so, many of the points in this chapter are worth considering. A chairman, for instance, may need to modify his approach if the general public are present, because they may not understand 'in' references.

Having decided the invitation to speak has come from a worthwhile source (and obviously you won't be able to be too choosy while trying to build up experience as a speaker) you need to know the day and date of the function to see if you can fit it in; always ask for both day *and* date because this avoids any confusion. If the date falls when you have a hectic business or social life planned, which will leave you with little time to prepare, then refuse the invitation rather than accept and have to do a rushed job. Be wary of using a clashing engagement as an excuse for saying 'no'; the organization may then offer alternative dates. If you don't want to speak, it is better to say so right at the start.

Having established 'who' and 'when', next you need to know 'where'. In your early speaking career it is unlikely your fame will have spread very far, so travelling will not be a problem; for functions further afield you need to establish if you can get there on time and, if you have no car, if you can do so by public transport.

However far the venue, get very specific directions for finding it, plus a phone number in case you break down or are delayed on the way. Many people are bad at giving directions and few will know road numbers, but do at least coax them to give you the name of a major landmark, such as a pub, near the venue. Good organizers should send you a map and advise you of complicated one-way systems; the more thoughtful ones will reserve a parking space for you and will have someone on the look-out when you arrive to make you feel welcome. But don't bank on it—the chairmen of local branches of well-known national organizations sometimes treat the arrival of a speaker as an unwelcome interruption to their chat with cronies.

During your discussions with the persons inviting you to speak, find out what arrangements will be made for accommodation, should you be travelling a reasonable distance to speak in the evening. Opt for a hotel if possible because although a stay with a committee member may be fine in the euphoria leading up to a function, it may be less so the next morning when the family is fighting with you for the bathroom.

It's a bit early in the book to mention it perhaps, but if you become a seasoned speaker you may need to consider what, if any, fee to charge. To save your blushes this sordid topic is covered later in the book (see page 115), although however amateur you are you should still be reimbursed with your expenses, unless of course you are anxious for the opportunity to speak in order to campaign over a particular issue.

Other things you need to know about a function include:

- *Arrangements for food*. If you eat on a train travelling to a function and then find that you are faced with a five-course meal, you may become too bloated to speak well. Find out in advance.

- *What dress is to be worn*. If it says 'dress optional' for a dinner, ask if the top table at least will be in evening dress and, if in doubt, tend to dress up not down when speaking. I fear I cannot advise you on dress if you are invited to speak at a nudists' function because, to my disappointment, I've never been invited to do so. They do say that you at least get an apparent round of applause when people sit down after drinking a toast you have proposed!

- *What time will it start?* Organizers usually expect you to arrive far too early, so try to establish a realistic start time—usually at least 15 minutes after that stated on a ticket, i.e. 7.30 for 8.00 p.m. means people will start slurping soup at around 8.15. If you plan to arrive later than the time suggested by the organizer, do tell him in advance otherwise you may arrive to find him under sedation for nervous exhaustion over your apparent non-arrival.

- *How long will you be expected to speak?* All organizers *under*-estimate how long raffles, official business and so on will take, while they *over*-estimate how long an audience will want to listen to you (especially if they are waiting for dancing to start). Even the time of day will affect the length of your speech. Breakfast meetings are dodgy affairs because few people are at their best first thing in the morning, while if you drone on too long after lunch you may hear the sound of chairs being pushed back as people leave. Some associations have a tradition of ending a meeting promptly at, say, 2.30 p.m. come what may, which may seem harsh on a speaker but does serve to concentrate the mind.

Having sorted out some or all of the above, it will help if the organizer puts it all in writing to you (efficient ones will do this anyway), and you should have business and home telephone numbers for your contact in the association.

Remember that you won't need much, if any, of the above detailed information if you are an honorary official speaking to your own association, while all the stress on attention to detail may also seem a bit over the top if you've just been asked to propose the loyal toast at a local association dinner. Nevertheless, for many functions you will need all of that information. For others you may need even more, for example:

- *Who were the speakers at the last function held by the organization and how well were they received*? This information will give you that all-important 'feel' for the audience and its expectations, particularly if the organizer says, for instance, 'We had old so-and-so and he went on for far too long.'

- *Who else is speaking and in what order*? This will save you going into shock on the day if you suddenly find you are sandwiched between two household names. If you feel the running order is wrong, for example because you know another of the speakers is brilliant and should therefore perform last, then suggest so to the organizer. A thoughtful organizer may send you a copy of the menu of the previous year's function which will help to give you the flavour of the occasion.

- *Will there be any auctions, raffles, prizegivings or traditional ceremonies held before you speak?* I was once about to get to my feet at a Round Table dinner when a host of pretty girls danced in wearing skimpy underwear. I'm not complaining, you understand, just pointing out the sort of thing that can happen; better to be forewarned. Similarly, it helps to know if any celebrities or even royalty will be present because they can distract an audience and disconcert you. (Try to close your mind to them.)

- *How many will there be in the audience and roughly what age and sex will they be?* A small audience will need a more intimate approach than a large one—you will have to 'pitch up' to make an impact on the latter. How sophisticated is it likely to be? Will it want a dry or broad approach?

- *Who are the members of the audience: are they there willingly, or have they been coerced by an over-enthusiastic club secretary?* A reader can turn a page (not yet) but a listener is stuck with you and may be less enthusiastic if he was dragooned into attending. Is the organization on a high or a low? Consider the differences in style needed, for example, if a sports club has won or lost. All these things will help you when planning your Gettysburg Address. Will all those present be members of the same group? If an association has had problems in selling tickets and 40 per cent of those present are guests, that means that only six out of ten will know, or care, what you are talking about if you get too technical on a subject relevant to that association. If partners are invited too then just 30 per cent or so may be remotely interested in what you are saying. See why all the background information is so important? You *must* have a feel for why an audience is there and what it is expecting of you. I still wince when I recall attempting a light-hearted address to a business lunch where the audience traditionally had a much more erudite 'lecture'. Not a success.

Obviously, it helps to know what you are supposed to be speaking about. Are you proposing a toast or responding to one? Are you there to amuse or inform? If you are considered an expert on some topic, don't settle for an organizer's invitation to 'Just give us twenty minutes or so on whatever you feel like.' Try to get a more specific brief. I've listened to a Euro MP speak for 25 minutes on a totally inappropriate theme to a trade association simply because he hadn't found out exactly which branch of the organization he was addressing and what interested them. (The subject he chose didn't.) Defining the topic becomes even more important for businessmen who are invited to give a keynote speech to a conference. (Incidentally, if you are asked to speak at a conference, try to resist requests to submit your speech weeks in advance—this is a sure way to extinguish any life in it.)

Give some thought to a title for your address if one is needed. The stronger the title, the bigger your audience is likely to be. 'How I made a million' will attract more people than 'How I founded Bloggs Builders'.

By making a nuisance of yourself to the organizer to find out all you can about your audience (and I can't stress its importance too highly) you will know whether your aim should be to inform, to motivate, or simply to entertain. If your objective is none of these but is to persuade them about an idea or thing—such as to lobby for or against something—then perhaps your speech should be only a part of a concerted approach. For example, if you are trying to stop a bypass and a politician is present, he will be more convinced of the depth of local feeling mentioned in your speech if he has passed posters in everyone's garden on his way to the hall. So do your spadework.

Business meetings

As if all that wasn't enough, businessmen speaking or making formal presentations need to go even further in audience analysis. For instance, if the audience is composed of customers then analyse their attitudes to you. Do you have close links with them and do they love your product? Or do they use your product but would be equally happy to use someone else's at a similar price? Maybe they are attending your presentation on sufferance and are, if anything, even unfriendly towards you? All this analysis could affect the tone of your presentation.

Traditional retailing patterns have changed dramatically in recent years (think of the hurly-burly in the banking world, for instance) and in many areas this has led to customers' loyalties breaking down. Don't assume that your customers are wedded to you for ever; don't treat them casually or bore them.

If you are presenting to a sales force, are sales buoyant or are things going badly? Are your representatives angry because you have chopped their discount or cut their allocation? All these things could affect the mood they arrive in. And if you leave for a meeting with a sales force whose members have travelled from around the country and you are burdened with head office problems, leave the problems in the car park. Your audience won't know, or want to know, about them; you should be thinking of motivating, not demoralizing.

You may say I've laboured the point about audience analysis too much. I make no apologies, because it is the key to successful speaking. In fact it is not too far-fetched to suggest that an audience can become one being; the more you know about the beast the better.

2
Preparation

Having analysed your audience as suggested in the previous chapter, you will probably be keen to sit down to write your golden words, but pause first and spend some time on *planning* what you are going to say. As you gain experience you will develop your own plan of action but, until then, follow this sequence: clarify your objectives— have a 'free-thinking' session—gather the information— sort it into a relevant order. (You will probably go through the sorting stage more than once.)

Accept from the start that you are very unlikely to change people's minds in a speech; what you may do is persuade them at least to consider your point of view. You may find it equally difficult to correct a well-entrenched falsehood (the 'big lie') but you may at least make people think twice and consider your alternative view.

Take care not to get out of your depth when speaking. Because of the power of the media we tend to deify too easily, and those who may be skilled or famous in one area, such as sport, are solemnly asked for their views on politics and, worse, they are sometimes unwise enough to pontificate and make fools of themselves in the process. Don't fall into the same trap. Stick to what you know because knowledge of a subject, however poorly pre- sented, is better than well-delivered waffle.

Once you have a clear idea of your objective in making a speech, take a notepad and 'free think' for a while; your first rough ideas, while you are perhaps still excited at having been invited to speak, may prove to be the best you will have on the subject. Just scribble down notes in no particular order. If you have been asked to speak on, say, buying and selling antiques, you might jot down 'treasures from attics' to remind you that a lay audience will be intrigued by a tale of someone who has stumbled on a valuable painting gathering dust somewhere. Similarly, 'rings' will remind you to include a piece on auctions, either confirming or demolishing the commonly held idea that dealers get together to rig things. You do not need to go into great depth during this free-thinking period—just make notes of general ideas.

The next stage is to gather information which will help you draft your speech. If your free-thinking session has indicated that some specific research will be needed, then put this in hand straight away even if your speech is not to be made for some time. Keep a box file or a desk drawer for all the various bits of information you accumulate— press clippings, leaflets, annual reports, tourist brochures, or whatever. The reference room at a local library will be a good source of information. Do *not* be tempted to shade or distort any facts or figures you use to support your case because if you do, someone in your audience will almost certainly know better and if that person corrects you in a question-and-answer session he will destroy your credibility. Don't be timid, however. If, for instance, some well-known or locally respected person supports your view and has been quoted in the press, then by all means use that as ammunition. Let's face it, lobbying for or against an issue such as a bypass could mean a lot to you so fire all the ammunition you can.

As well as using your local library, you may also accumulate a few reference books of your own. A thesaurus will be useful if you are trying to construct a deft turn of phrase (don't make it too convoluted) and a dictionary and, perhaps, an encyclopaedia will be worth having to hand. If you wish to quote from the Bible a concordance will steer you to a suitable quotation on almost any subject. In assembling information for a speech you will almost certainly acquire too much (the event organizer, for instance, may send you reams of brochures and back-up leaflets), so sift through for the really relevant material and throw the rest away.

Having gathered your information, you come to your first 'sort'. Go through everything you have accumulated, the bulk of which should be slips of paper with your own thoughts on them, and then grade the material into:

- Essential facts which your audience *must* have.
- Information which they *should* know.
- Material which it would be nice for them to know but which is not essential.

Sorting the information in this way will clarify your thinking and will help if you have to delete material because your speech is too long (and most are). At this point you will begin to appreciate that the hardest part of public speaking is not getting to your feet to deliver your speech, but putting your backside on a seat to plan it. Force yourself to go through this stage because it is vital to success. And—as if you could forget—do keep your audience in mind at all times. Consider too what their attitude to you is likely to be—and don't assume that they will know you. A bit player on a long-running television soap may be instantly recognized by part of an audience, but be totally unknown to the rest. If you come into this category, make sure the chairman has enough biographical information to introduce you properly and then avoid using too much 'in' material which may be incomprehensible to a large section of your audience.

At this stage in your planning, you may find it helpful to jot down the key points you plan to make on to cards—perhaps a printer's cheap offcuts, roughly postcard size. The advantage with such cards is that you can shuffle the points around to improve the flow of what you plan to say. You can, of course, use a sheet of paper and jot numbers against the notes as you clarify your thinking but cards make the process easier. Do not confuse the rough notes made at this stage with the memory aids.

Logically, you could sort your notes into the following order: an introduction; the points you want to make; arguments to support your case; perhaps a brief note of any opposition view (being careful to demolish it, of course); a summing up.

I said 'logically' but, of course, no two occasions are the

same. If you were lecturing on the life of the house sparrow you would hardly need to be 'arguing' too strongly about anything. Equally, if making an after-dinner speech proposing the toast of an association, you would rarely be quoting opposition views; although if you were addressing, say, solicitors and wanted to wake them up you could refer to the growth of self-conveyancing before coming down in their favour (always supposing that is your genuine view—steer clear of the subject if it isn't).

Whatever the occasion your planning must aim to make your speech flow, and ideally it should have a theme to tie it all together; your audience will be confused if you bob about without any logical links. Having the information on separate cards will help you to sort things into a logical sequence; after a first canter through you may decide on a 'second sort' in which you rejig the running order either mildly or entirely. For example, the 'first sort' for the aforementioned speech on buying and selling antiques might put the attic treasure reference towards the end. The 'second sort' might bring it to the front as an attention-grabbing introduction, perhaps along the following lines: 'Last week an old lady brought into my antique shop a bowl which she had found in an old suitcase in her attic. I gave her £4,000 for it.' No-one will go to sleep after that, but not many will believe you either.

Let me stress again the key point—**remember the audience**. People won't want a second-hand speech, they will want *your* views so try to being something fresh to a subject. Pinching other people's ideas and dressing them up as your own is really not the done thing, apart from jokes, that is, because it is quite common to see members of an audience writing down a speaker's jokes. I'm not sure what they do with them afterwards but it doesn't matter too much anyway because humour is as much a matter of delivery and timing as content.

To summarize: you've found out all you can about your audience; you've dug out some facts and sorted them into roughly the right order; you've gone through again and put them into an even more attractive order to give a better flow. You are now ready to write your speech.

3
Drafting a speech

If you have time, take a break between your initial preparation and writing your speech down because you may have useful second thoughts; if there is anything which you cannot understand when you look at your rough notes later, you will obviously have to change it if your audience is to follow you.

When drafting your speech, use the cards with jotted notes mentioned in the previous chapter but add more detailed comments such as a link between one point and the next; we will look at the actual paperwork you will use to remember it all 'on the day' in the next chapter.

The quality of your speech results from the style you impart to it. There is little point in including 'set' speeches in a book like this because circumstances vary too much, but there are some things to watch for whatever the occasion:

- *Have something to say* Obvious? Of course it is but an awful lot of speakers seem to use words just to fill up the time.

- *Don't be stuffy* You may be deeply interested in the minutiae of your subject, but don't assume others will be or you may not hold their attention.

- *Don't pretend to be more knowledgeable than you really are* You won't be too audible if you talk through your hat.

- *Don't string a series of platitudes and clichés together and expect it to rate as a speech* It will just be soporific.

- *Try to bring light and shade to a speech* An even pace and tone can be monotonous.

- *Don't be a poseur* Be yourself.

- *Don't talk up or down to an audience.*

- *Don't be afraid to admit your mistakes, perhaps to illustrate a point* It will make you seem that much more human and your audience will warm to you.

- *Involve your audience whenever you can* For instance, if you are lobbying for a bypass, a comment such as, 'If traffic flow continues through the high street at the present rate, in eight years' time one in three of the houses will need major repairs and we will *all* face doubled insurance premiums,' will hold people's attention.

- *Use actual examples to illustrate points whenever you can* They will hold attention better than generalities.

- *Take people behind the scenes of your job or hobby* For instance, if you are in the legal profession give your audience an insight into what old judges do at the end of lengthy court cases. If you are in show business they will love a bit of gossip, although clearly you should not be slanderous or too indiscreet, especially if the media are present.

- *Don't ride pet hobby horses too long or too hard* You will just make your audience saddle-sore.

- *Try to make your speech apt* If you are presenting school prizes, don't talk for 20 minutes on land drainage or you will bore everyone. And, whatever you do, don't patronize children.

With these points in mind, you should start building your speech by framing a strong introduction. To some extent as a speaker you have to 'control' an audience and to do this you first have to get its attention, which is why a good introduction is so important.

If you are unknown to an audience you may consider a shock approach to grab attention, although attitudes change. Standing up and starting with, *'I am a lesbian,'* would still take courage before some audiences, and you would still need caution if saying, 'I was a bank robber,' before going on to sell life assurance. But to start a talk on gambling by announcing, 'I won (or lost) £5,000 last week,' would assure you of close attention.

Having drafted your introduction, jot down notes to tell the audience what you are planning to do. For example, 'I would like to talk about the new bypass and the damage it will do to valuable farmland. I will then explain how an alternative line would cause less disruption and still retain the playing fields.' On the day proceed to do just that and end by recapping your main points.

If you have a very strong introduction, the letdown will be all the greater if it is followed by a poor speech. Nevertheless don't necessarily put your key message right after your introduction; gain the audience's confidence first.

When you do come to your 'message' (always supposing you have one) make quite sure that the audience understands it. Don't wrap it up so warmly with generalities that no-one spots it, nor cloud an issue just because it is a sad one. Don't waffle on about the benefits to a village of this and that if the real crux is that a playing field is to be dug up. Always assume that you will be found out if you take this approach, and when you are you will be seen as devious.

As you draft the body of your speech you may need to rejig your note cards yet again to improve the flow but whatever the final running order, include 'signposts' between the sections so that you carry an audience with you. People are most comfortable when they know what is going on, so say such things as 'So that is the effect on jobs; now I would like to look at the effect on housing.'

Few of us in general conversation give much thought to our choice of words or spend time 'orating' (our friends would consider us unhinged if we did) but for a speech try to build in a rhythm, occasionally even a 'rhythm of three': 'We are going to do this, we are going to do that and we are going to do the other.' But in your search for eloquence beware of a rhythm that will make you sound like William

McGonagall, the Scottish poet noted for his bad verse:
'There were cries of delight, in the valleys last night.' I am
sure you can see the danger.

To strengthen a point, you may decide to argue *against*
it, for example: 'I believe the changes will improve the
amenities of the village, but it can be argued that they will
in fact destroy them because . . .' Don't, however, labour
the point and avoid too much of 'on the one hand . . . on
the other'. The audience wants to hear *your* views,so you
should put them across sooner rather than later.

To create shock waves and keep people awake, you may
decide to butcher a few sacred cows. Addressing a bunch
of boffins, you could say 'The computer is turning us into
a race of souless zombies and the idea that we need one in
every home to record accounts and addresses is quite
ludicrous.' If this is too bold for you, try a more cowardly
approach: 'Some people argue that . . .' followed by what
may be the unpopular view. If the audience jeers, quickly
move on to the opposite view or, if there is no reaction,
say, '. . . and I agree with them!' Then take cover.

When taking a controversial approach, be wary of
attacking the cherished traditions of an association or of
over-strong attacks on famous people (even politicians),
because you may offend some of your audience. Mock
yourself by all means; in fact it is far better to do this than
to praise yourself or your company or association, unless
you do this by way of obvious overstatement. For
instance, if you get up at a Round Table and say that you
represent table number such and such 'which is, of
course, the best in the area' you will get ribald jeers but
they will be fairly friendly ones.

After telling you what to do, it is time for a few things to
guard against:

- *Avoid superlatives.* Particularly so in connection with
  your own efforts or products.

- *Mix short and long sentences to add variety but avoid
  desperately convoluted ones.* Short ones will be more
  readily understood and will make a greater impact.
  If you use a long sentence, try not to leave the verb
  until the end because an audience may lose your

thread if it has to wait too long for the 'action' word.

- *If you use a long word, get it right* Look it up in a dictionary if you are not sure. Even if you get it correct you are likely to get a sarcastic 'ooh' from someone (as you may if you quote some utterly obscure historical figure, because they will know you looked it up).

- *Steer clear of phrases like 'at this point in time' if you mean 'now'* I'm sure you've heard many similar examples but that one has the most currency and is certainly the most jarring.

- *Acknowledge your sources* Particularly if you are speaking to a specialist audience, because they may have read the same newspaper or magazine article.

As an aside, if you are privileged to receive an invitation to speak to a foreign audience, find someone of that nationality to steer you clear of the obvious pitfalls and introduce you to their customs. Obviously you should delete any 'in' references or comments about domestic television programmes because they won't be understood. What you *must* do is say a few words in their language, either of welcome or in proposing a toast. Write your words in English, get someone to translate them and say them into a tape recorder for you, then write your own phonetic interpretation of what is on the tape. Your notes can be total gibberish provided they sound like the foreign language when you read them. Then rehearse. I followed these instructions for a 15-minute speech in a language I don't speak and was congratulated on my accent.

Whatever the nationality of the audience you should avoid complicated figures or statistics unless you are addressing a specialist group. Although it will be simpler to use even numbers whenever you can—1,100 not 1,099 or 1,101—keep in mind that a whole number, say 8 per cent, may look like an estimate or guess whereas 8.1 per cent seems somehow more accurate. However, I'm not suggesting you should shade the truth in using such techniques. Incidentally, it is probably better to under-rather than overstate such things as sales forecasts. Don't make hostages to fortune. Far better in a year's time to be able to say that a target was beaten than missed.

Paint word pictures of statistics to make them more easily understood: 'four times the size of this room' is more readily grasped than so many square metres or feet. Incidentally, for some years yet you should assume that metric figures will result in glazed looks among older members of a British or American audience. Finally, on statistics, if something seems totally unbelievable, say something like 'Yes, I know that sounds impossible but I've double-checked it and . . .' Try to remember the following advice too:

- *Avoid clichés* This book only uses them to illustrate how awful they sound, of course.

- *Avoid giving undue offence* I once saw a function wrecked because a speaker unthinkingly referred to someone who had made a mistake as a 'spastic' and a listener in a wheelchair made for the door. Apart from political meetings and the glorious rumbustiousness of Speakers' Corner, your audience will not expect to be offended; take care not to do so.

- *Beware of jargon, attempts at current slang, or 'in'-talk* A middle-aged person wrestling with youngsters' language is as comical as an ageing disc jockey. Dig?

- *Don't use foreign phrases unless you know the audience will understand them* They will either confuse or sound patronizing.

- *Don't use abbreviations.* Abbreviations such as GNP (Gross National Product), GRP and so on, and even percentages may not always be understood. Avoid them, or simplify and say seven out of ten people rather than 70 per cent. 'GRP' may be understood as glass-reinforced plastic by non-economists.

- *Avoid name-dropping* It will just make an audience wince, as I was saying to Prince Charles only the other day.

- *Ask a friend to tell you if you have the irritating habit of saying 'I mean' or 'like', then try to stop yourself* The most common is 'you know'. If they know, why bother telling them?

Having avoided all those pitfalls and having put your note cards in the right order with explanatory or linking comments on them, go through and delete any waffle or unnecessary distractions from the main theme of your speech. Then step back and take a detached view of whether you have a logical form to your speech with a thread running through it.

Now draft your final section. You may say: 'So let me sum up,' and hit your key points again. On the day, if you can think on your feet restate anything which you felt was misunderstood or which got an adverse reaction. Add something like: 'I know you jeered when I said such and such; well let me just remind you that . . .' Incidentally, if you recap on your main points at the end, it may help to rephrase some of them to introduce a fresh line, although if you have a slogan to put across then obviously you should not tamper with it.

Having finished the notes for your concluding section, take one final detached look at it all, remembering that your message is not what you think you have said but what your audience takes away with them. If people cannot understand something they have read they can look at it again but they only have one chance with your spoken word, which is why planning is so important. If you haven't assembled your thoughts properly, you have little chance of being understood.

I mentioned earlier that you should include 'signposts' in a speech to carry the audience with you. As an example, here is a signpost to indicate where we are in this book. We have seen how important it is to learn all you can about an audience. We have considered how to assemble facts on rough note cards and how to sort them into the right order, and we've looked at how to construct a speech using those facts. Now let us look at what, if any, memory aids you will need.

4
Memory joggers

If you are a disciplined and clear thinker then the rough notes suggested so far may suffice as memory aids for a speech, but this is unlikely because they may now be covered with scribbles. So let us examine what memory aids you could make using the rough notes as a basis.

If you are unsure of yourself, having a speech written out in full will calm your nerves and get you through the ordeal without much difficulty. If you do a lot of speaking you could even put your comments on to a word processor and select key bits for particular speeches, but be careful that this doesn't make all your speeches sound sterile and stale.

Although reading a speech will certainly get you through it, there are pitfalls. For example, it is difficult to write words to be spoken. Few people say 'it is raining'; they say 'it's raining,' so use the shorter version when writing out a speech. Saying your words into a tape recorder and then writing them down from a playback may help. Incidentally, if you have the luxury of dictating your speech to a skilled secretary, abbreviating things to 'it's' and 'that's' will not come naturally, so explain why you want it written in this way. Typed notes should be double-spaced in upper and lower case, not capitals, throughout as the latter can be difficult to read. (Consider a machine with a large typeface if you have poor vision.) Incidentally, don't worry too much about grammar; your task is to be understood, which means speaking the language used in everyday life, so split infinitives if you wish and hang the purists.

If you are going to read your speech, watch page turnover points. When you are in full cry over a key point, turning over a page may disturb your flow and could, if you turn over two pages by mistake, wreck a point completely. You may decide to underline or mark key pieces in colour, but don't overdo it or your bouts of emphasis will sound too regular and forced.

Writing out a speech sounds easy and less nerve-racking than other methods. Maybe, but sheaves of paper can dismay an audience, especially if you take forever before turning over the first one. Above all, the snag with reading from a script is that it will be very difficult to make it sound natural. Work hard to use spoken, not written phrases; delete any unnecessary words and smooth out any tortuous sections.

Cueing systems are increasingly being used whereby a speaker looks at his audience through one or more sheets of glass (which for some speakers should really be bullet-proof). A speech is typed on to a paper roll then projected up and on to a glass in front of the speaker. Someone out of sight turns the roll at the right pace for the presenter. The result is that the speaker sees every word of his speech while looking at an audience, which only sees clear glass. This method is obviously much better for eye contact than putting your head down to read a speech, although fluffs tend to look strange while a breakdown in the system becomes positively surrealistic. It takes a little while to get used to reading only a few words per line on the prompt role—have a practice run if possible. Such systems are likely to be out of the reach of social organizations and anyway are quite unnecessary for most of their functions, and at business meetings you will still be reading your words with the resultant lack of naturalness.

You may, of course, simply have to read a fully written-out speech if a number of visuals need cueing in—many conference presentations are read for just this reason. A further advantage is that the approximate length is known in advance for timing a meeting.

Instead of laboriously writing out a whole speech, you may consider using 'bullet points' for part of it. Bullets are short key words or phrases to remind you what to say. I am not suggesting for one moment that you should actually fire anything at an audience; you must use other skills to keep them awake.

As an example of the bullet system you might write:

- Honoured: five years
- Village hall/ballroom
- Message same.

To remind you to say: 'I am honoured to be speaking to you tonight. It is five years since I was last here and I recall then you met in the village hall, not in this magnificent ballroom. But my message is still the same . . .' then read your key message. Even if your opening words prove less elegant than if carefully written out beforehand, they will still sound a lot more sincere. Similarly, you could end your notes with a few key words to remind you to wish them well in their fund-raising, and then propose a toast.

If you decide to try this system of 'part bullets, part written in full', you may construct your notes by editing down from a fully written-out speech, but be careful because highlighting a few key words or phrases in a fully written copy of your text to use as bullet points will probably confuse you. Better to prepare fresh notes.

The most spontaneous delivery of all is likely to result from using just bullet points for your entire speech. How detailed the bullets should be will depend on your confidence and subject knowledge. If you were making a speech on 'making a speech' you might prepare bullets as follows:

- Define objectives
- Inform, lobby or entertain?
- Jot down points to make
- Collect supporting information
- Sort into logical order
- Draft outline
- Prepare notes.

These bullets would enable you to take your audience through some of the stages in preparing a speech. With more confidence you could abbreviate the notes even further to:

- Objectives
- Inform, lobby, entertain?
- Points to make
- Back-up info
- Sort
- Outline
- Notes.

If you go too far in paring down your notes you may stumble once or twice in your first delivery, but your speech will be sharper and more alive than if you'd read it. Space out your notes so that you can add afterthoughts if, for example, an earlier speaker mentions a point you would like to pick up. I often find that having prepared very scanty bullet points I put back more detailed comments just before I speak, which I know is simply through nerves.

You may develop a system of using capital letters for key sections of your speech, with sub-headings to cover back-up points. Do whatever turns you on (see the earlier point about how silly such slang sounds) and, above all, calms you down.

If you know your subject well and have a series of slides or flipovers to illustrate your presentation, you may be able to dispense with notes altogether and let your visuals remind you of what you want to say. (As a safeguard, you could lightly pencil a few notes on the corner of a flipover chart.) This method can give a very relaxed air to a talk and demonstrate that the speaker is totally in command of his subject. If you start to dry up over a particular visual just move on to the next as a memory jogger. It is worth having bullet notes to hand as a safety net until you are confident enough to use just the visuals as notes.

You may think that learning a speech by heart will result

in the best delivery, but it won't. It is very hard work and unless you are a trained actor the audience will still sense that you are 'reading' your speech, although in the back of your mind not on a sheet of paper. Drying up or losing your way can be disastrous, while if another speaker uses a point you planned to make it may be difficult to modify your carefully memorized words. Above all, you may be concentrating so much on what you are going to say that you will find it almost impossible to react to an audience. If, despite these awful warnings, you *do* decide to memorize a speech, at least have a copy of the script in your pocket or on the table. It will give you added confidence.

If you are repeating a speech you have already given several times before or you know your subject extremely well, then by all means get up and speak without notes—provided you are doing it from the heart and using fresh, not carefully memorized, words each time.

To summarize: unless you plan to get your message across by thought transference or mass hypnosis, I strongly recommend that you use bullet points as memory joggers when giving a speech or talk.

Whatever form of memory aid you have, do use firm paper. If you have sheaves of flimsy paper and are nervous, your slightest tremble will show as the notes wave about. If this becomes too obvious, announce that you are waving the paper about as a temporary measure because the air conditioning has failed. Some platitudinous (and there's a word you'd be foolish to use in front of many audiences) speakers could almost have packs of 'cliché cards' to be shuffled without noticeable effect on the result. You should avoid having so many cards that it looks as if you are going to do conjuring tricks or that the audience is in for a long haul.

Loose cards should be large enough to be handled easily, yet small enough to go into a pocket or handbag. They *must* be numbered, and ideally, strung together with a cord through holes punched in the top left-hand corners.

I dislike books in which an author imposes too much of 'I' this and 'I' that on his readers, but I ask you to bear with me here while I describe the way I make the notes I use because I think it is a better system than loose cards.

I rarely speak for more than 20 minutes (I'm kind to dumb animals as well as audiences) and work from very brief bullet points. I use sheets of card (slightly thinner than postcards) which are A4 width – 8 inches (21 cm) – and about the same in depth. I fold the sheets once so that in effect I have four columns, 4 inches (10½ cm) wide by 8 inches (21 cm) deep. Why this size? Because the card will slip easily into the inside pocket of a man's jacket or a woman's handbag. With the card folded I write '1' at the top of the first sheet and jot my bullet points down and then (remembering the point about turning at a convenient part of the speech) I start the second column, being careful to number that too. I try to find a suitable point or, if I'm lucky, a laughter pause, for the bottom of page 2 to give me time to refold the card so that columns 3 and 4 are on the outside ready to be used. For a speech of up to 20 minutes my bullets usually end about half-way down the fourth column. I draw a line under my final bullet (often the toast to be proposed) and then in the spare space jot down points which I could substitute for any in my speech used by a preceding speaker. I've never needed more than one of the cards.

I hope you are still with me. The advantage with my method, which I am sure countless other speakers use too, is that even if you drop such a card the 'pages' can't get out of order because they are all on a single piece of card. Making a speech fit on no more than four columns (preferably less) acts as a useful time discipline too.

When you've completed your notes, consider pencilled brackets round points which can be deleted if you are not making any headway with your audience. Consider colour coding your notes too: red for things you must say, yellow for things you can skip, and so on. There is no recommended system for this, just do whatever you feel happy with.

I carry a spare copy of my note card, written on ordinary paper, just in case I hack the first one about before speaking. I can then make a more legible set of notes by modifying the spare set. I hardly ever need to do this and I know carrying the spare is a nervous mannerism

but I can't stop.
  Two final tips:

- Be wary of putting gesture cues in your notes because the results may look staged. We will cover delivering a speech later in the book (see pages 88-94), but if you need to put a note to tell you to turn to the chairman when you are actually speaking about him, then I reckon you've got problems as a speaker which no book will cure.

- Having prepared your notes, add key information such as the address of the venue, the name of the person to contract and so on, and then either file or throw away any supporting material you've accumulated; you won't be using it during your speech.

5
Protocol

When asked to make a speech or simply propose a toast, people often get worried about protocol—how they should address the lord mayor and so on. This concern is quite unnecessary because if a dignatory is present he, or an aide, will tell you the right form, as will any competent toast-master. You won't go far wrong over forms of address if you list people in roughly their order of importance, (although their feeling of self-importance may differ from your assessment). You should acknowledge the senior person present by opening with: 'Mr Chairman (or Mr President), ladies and gentlemen'. If you refer to other people by name, either at this point (say, for a particularly honoured guest) or during your speech, make an effort to get things right. It is discourteous to call Mr Wilson, Mr Watson, or vice versa.

If a 'Sir' is present and you wish to refer to him, drop the surname—call Sir John Smith 'Sir John'. If a Mayor is present, call him or her 'Mr Mayor' or 'Madam Mayor'. Incidentally, the chairman is always mentioned first unless royalty is present. If you are speaking in front of the Queen (one can dream), begin: 'May it please Your Majesty, Mr Chairman . . .' If other royals are present, you should start: 'May it please your Royal Highness, Mr Chairman . . .' In America, obviously you would refer to Mr President (if he were there) before Mr Chairman, and so on. There are other 'rules' for senior church figures and for lords, dukes and others. Ask the toast-master or others for advice on the day. A good organizer will even put a slip of paper in front of speakers with the suggested form of introduction on it.

The shortest 'speech' you are likely to make is if you are asked to say grace. Where possible grace should be said before guests sit down so that they are not disturbed immediately they have settled in their seats. You don't have to stand for grace, but it would be a bold organizer who suggested otherwise because the convention is so strong that guests may be confused—people are happier when they are comfortable with what is happening.

If you are asked to say grace try to come up with something more original that 'For what we are about to receive may the Lord make us truly thankful.' A clergyman once said: 'Bless the chef and all who serve us. From indigestion Lord, preserve us,' after which everyone sat down smiling.

The Selkirk Grace, which is attributed to Robert Burns, always makes a nice start to a meal, although it really needs the right accent to deliver it properly.

> Some hae meat, and canna eat,
> And some wad eat that want it,
> But we hae meat and we can eat,
> And sae the Lord be thankit.

If you feel your audience will accept it, you could try the following:

> Gentle Jesus, Lord Divine
> Who turneth water into wine,
> Please forgive these foolish men
> Who seek to turn it back again.

In striving to be original, it is acceptable to say something like: 'Bless our food, our friendship and the aims of our association' but don't go too far in this direction. Don't include a plug for a product or ask people to pray for the downfall of an opposing team at a sports dinner.

I've seen a poster of a prayer found on the wall of an old inn:

> Give us, Lord, a bit o'sun,
> a bit o'work and a bit o'fun;

give us all in the struggle and sputter
our daily bread and a bit o'butter.

Those lines would make rather a nice grace.

Without wishing to over-dramatize the saying of grace,
it is often the first thing said during an evening, so
remember that if you can produce something apt and
original you will get things off to a fine start.

Even shorter than a grace is the loyal toast. Here, no
speech is required, in fact to make one would be quite
wrong. Usually the chairman or president just says: 'The
Queen'. The master of ceremonies, the toast-master or the
chairman himself should ask guests to 'be upstanding'
before you propose the toast.

Other toasts may occur during a meal before the formal
speeches and toasts. If beef is piped in, it is customary for
the senior person present to toast the piper, which means
having a couple of glasses ready; Scots may wish to
'address the haggis'. If you are involved in such things, do
resist the temptation to go on too long.

At some associations it is customary for the chairman
(and his lady) to 'take wine with . . .' various sections of
the audience. This is appropriate with, say, 'all the
founder members' when an association is celebrating a
significant anniversary but, as with all activities like this, it
should not be so overdone as to become tiresome.

Eventually, you will arrive at the more usual toasts.
Someone will propose a toast to an association, a senior
member will respond, after which the chairman will
propose 'the guests', with a response by a fourth speaker.
Sadistic or over-enthusiastic organizers will prolong
things with an extra couple of toasts; more caring ones
(perhaps because they are unable to find enough
speakers) will have the chairman respond to the first toast
and continue to propose the guests so that there are only
three speeches.

If you are one of the speakers then concentrate on your
main presentation and don't worry too much about the
protocol in your introduction. Traditions are jolly nice and
we should deplore the decline in standards, but don't take
it all too seriously and certainly don't let yourself get

worked up about it. If you get the order wrong the only ones to notice will be the people you relegate in the batting order and if such a trivial thing upsets them, they can't be all that important, can they?

6
Talks and lectures

So far this book had been directed at those making speeches, such as at a social organization's annual dinner, but the same principles apply if you are giving a talk or lecture. Few dictionaries are clear on the difference between the two, but if you were addressing a general audience on woodland mammals it could be described as a talk, whereas an address to biology students on the nervous system of small vertebrates would be a lecture. Talks are likely to be given to those who are interested, however mildly, in a subject; lectures are often directed at those who know something about a subject and want, or need, to know more. Lectures tend to be more 'formal' and are expected to inform more than talks which may be quite general; both perhaps appeal more to the intellect than the emotions as a public speech would do.

If talks and lectures are to inform, then it follows that if you are to deliver one you need to know your subject. Anyone can propose a toast to an association because anyone can dig out a few things to say before asking people to raise their glasses. Not everyone can, or should, stand up and talk or lecture on Rennaissance art. No-one should talk or lecture without a reasonable knowledge of the subject. If they've only read a couple of books and try to bluff their way through, you can be sure that there will be someone far more erudite in the audience who will be itching to air his knowledge by asking questions, to the speaker's discomfort.

Lectures should not be prepared in isolation. Consider what has gone before, either on the day or at the previous function held by the group. A series of lectures should be planned as a whole and an organizer should have briefed you that you are following Mr Jones who will be speaking on such-and-such. If your such-and-such is similar to his, you may need to contact him to avoid duplication. Ideally, an organizer should plan a series of lectures so that there is light and shade—a procession of very heavy topics will stupefy even the most learned audience. Lectures should be connected by 'bridges', either by a chairman linking the various speakers or by you, at the start of your address, saying something like 'Mr Jones looked at housing; I'd like to move outside and consider roads.

If lecturing, try to sit at the back for the lecture immediately preceding yours in order to get a feel for an audience. That is also why I suggest that you should find out what has gone on at the previous function held by the organization. If someone went down well talking about a very obscure topic, it may give you a pointer as to how serious you need to be. If you know one of the previous speakers, ring him to get his views of the association—it may be very different from the secretary's.

You will have to pay even more attention to your preparation if you are billed to give a keynote speech or lecture. These are supposed to strike at the heart of the topic with other presentations being complementary. Although you must obviously state your own views on such occasions, check with the organizers to see if they are anxious to have particular points put across; it would be discourteous not to refer to them at least.

Many scientific bodies like to have lectures supplied well in advance; some even issue them and then the members sit politely while lecturers read through them. If you find yourself in this bizarre situation, try to freshen your address with an occasional ad lib, although take care that you don't then lose your thread and find difficulty in returning to the main body of your address.

Frankly, many lectures regurgitate old information and some lecturers do get very stale. (Listen to what children say about their teachers.) This even applies to business conferences where the audience has paid to attend, although this may not be totally disastrous because the exchange of views over coffee or lunch may be just as valuable to attendees as what they hear in a lecture hall. Nevertheless, if you are invited to lecture do try to bring something fresh or thought-provoking to the subject.

7
Business presentations

Just as talks and lectures need a slightly different approach to 'normal' speeches, so do business presentations. To be effective in making one you must carefully match the presentation to the audience and strike a balance between excessive modesty and going hopelessly over the top. The same harmony is important if, instead of selling something, you are communicating with or trying to motivate employees.

The first step in making a presentation is to set clear objectives. Strangely, organizations which routinely set precise goals for many of their activities often let their standards slip when it comes to presenting a new product or service to the market-place. This is unbusinesslike because the launch is a vital link in the chain leading to the consumer. Too often a presentation to retailers or staff will be made without proper planning, yet only a little attention to detail is needed to make a dramatic difference to the success of such a meeting.

Seminars, symposia, workshops, conferences, meetings . . . whatever the business function, the first thing to do is vow *never* to hold such a meeting just for the sake of it; you must have a more clearly defined purpose. Even if you have relatively little control over where and when, because you are presenting to a customer and may be at his beck and call, you should still plan your approach carefully to maximize your chances of success. For meetings initiated by you, ask yourself if you are really just calling people together because it is an annual tradition. This is not a strong enough reason. Getting people together costs money—quite a lot of it if you include salaries, travel and entertaining, not to mention lost sales while your representatives are quaffing your coffee—so set clear objectives for meetings. And write them down. Don't be too bland; it is too easy to settle for an important-sounding but meaningless objective, just as many company creeds come close to waffling on about motherhood and kindness to animals. Try to quantify what you are hoping to achieve and if, say, you are telling employees about the benefits of being paid by cheque, write down what percentage you hope will switch from cash.

Writing down your objectives will help to establish whether you are trying to inform, sell, motivate or entertain in your presentation; although you should really try to do the latter, whatever your other aims, to stop your audience going to sleep. Launching a new product? Well, if *you* don't make a song and dance about it, rest assured that no-one else will; and if you don't shout about it to motivate the sales force, then they may think you are not very excited by it and conclude that it can't be very good.

Whatever the presentation, be clear what messages you are trying to get across and don't have too many or you will just confuse your audience. You are unlikely to change people's minds during a presentation. You may persuade them that a new product has merit, but if retailers are convinced that your discount structure is out of line with your competitors then only drastic action and/or a very plausible presentation is likely to convince them otherwise. Accept too that it will be difficult to shift a well-entrenched falsehood. If your company has had grossly unfair coverage in the press, you will have to work very hard to overcome the conclusion 'Yes, but there's no smoke . . .'

In your initial planning decide what information flow you want at the presentation. Is it to be one-way, with you presenting to the audience? Well, if so, only your golden words stand between it and slumber. Where appropriate it is better to have a two-way exchange of views, perhaps via meetings of subgroups, such as engineers or salesmen, after a main presentation.

As well as considering your objectives in making a business presentation, consider too the venue (discussed in more detail in *Thorsons Guide to Making Business Presentations*) because the environment in which you present will send out strong signals about your organization. If the place is scruffy or noisy and the projector doesn't work . . . well, draw your own conclusions. Your guests certainly will.

Setting objectives and finding a suitable venue are all important but preparing the words for a presentation is still perhaps the most important thing of all. If you don't get it right your message may fall flat. Follow much the same sequence described in Chapter 2, namely: sit back and generally think about the subject matter; collect necessary information; sort this information into the right order; then write the words. If you are trying to sell a customer something in a face-to-face meeting you may feel that all those stages are unnecessary, but they are not. Reflect on what the customer will be expecting; are there any problems with existing products he is likely to raise? Collect any information you may need to support your case and even if you don't write it down, consider how to present the information in such a way as to make an impact. Give some thought to which words you will use.

Remember that a successful presentation must have something to say, such as the advantages your product offers the customer. Most businessmen don't like wasting time so, having made them welcome, you should say what is going to happen at the meeting. Keep in mind that not everyone will want a highly technical presentation. Have detailed information available, of course, and touch on the highlights but if, for example, you are trying to sell a new air-conditioning system, details of cost and ease of operation may be more important than a technical lecture on how it works. If you designed it yourself you may be deeply interested in this but don't assume anyone else will be.

Initially you are likely to be using fully typed-out words for business presentations. When presenting from a lectern your words can be written on ordinary sheets of paper, but not so deep that you have to bury your chin in your chest to read the bottom lines. Incidentally, whatever memory system you use, change the running order if you think it will make your presentation more effective; the only time you need care is if you have a lot of carefully cued visual aids.

As you gain confidence in speaking you may find it far better to put things behind you and work from the 'bullet points' referred to earlier (see pages 31-32). This system is likely to make your presentation much more lively and natural than if you read it. If you intend to talk about market trends then a bullet saying '1st quarter 26%, 2nd quarter 28%' may be all you need to remind you about how sales moved in the first half of a year. That bullet could be cut to '1Q:26, 2Q:28' or phrased in other ways—you will rapidly develop your own shorthand system. Double- or treble-space the bullets so that there is room between them to add other notes as the meeting progresses.

All the above assumes that you are giving your own business presentation but the choice of presenters to deliver information is so critical that if, say, you are the boss of a small company and, being honest with yourself, know that you are better on the shop floor than at selling, you could simply welcome your audience before handing over to someone else to do the actual sales pitch.

You may consider an unusual approach when selecting presenters. I've seen a chef come out of a kitchen to give a marvellous address to a food company's sales force. (He had been tactful enough to use that firm's products in preparing a meal the sales force had just enjoyed.) Avoid sketches featuring company personnel, no matter how keen they are on amateur dramatics; most of them will be acutely embarrassing. Be equally cautious with two-handed presentations. These are less dangerous than sketches, but still need great care if they are not to sound forced. Give each speaker a minute or two at a time rather than one or two sentences because the flow will be smoother where there are fewer change points to be fluffed. Balance the running order between heavyweight and lighter subjects, remembering at the same time to follow a logical sequence. A speaker who is known to be humorous would be best at the end of the presentation, otherwise following speakers may come as an anticlimax.

A brief informal chat over coffee before a presentation commences may help to break the ice. When the meeting starts, identify yourself and your colleagues, with one-line comments if necessary; for example, 'Roger has just put in our new control system,' or 'Mary has joined us from ABC Ltd.' After the introductions, let your audience know what is going to happen and whether questions are expected during the presentation or are to be held until the end; the latter is preferable with a structured presentation to avoid getting side-tracked or pre-empting what is to come. State whether there are to be any hand-outs and, if not, have pads available in case people wish to make notes.

If you go to a theatre you have presumably chosen to see the show and therefore you go with some anticipation and are ready to be entertained; the audience at your presentation may be there under mild duress so expect less warmth at the start. Television shows use warm-up men to relax the audience beforehand; I'm not suggesting you should put on a funny mask, but at least make your opening remarks warm and friendly. Your audience should be ready to listen before you put your key message across.

Once your presentation is underway it all hinges on 'style'. Say enough, but know when to stop talking. Behavioural scientists will tell you which words to avoid and how to study body language but even if you have not risen to that lofty level, you *should* be able to tell if you are boring the pants off your audience or if it is getting irritated by what you are saying. Unfortunately it appears that not everyone can, which is why after-dinner speakers persist in droning on when their audience has long since stopped listening. With a business meeting—where sales could be at risk, for instance—it is absolutely vital that you tailor things to your audience and try to be flexible enough to change tack during your presentation if you sense that it is not going well.

If you know that a certain problem will be raised by a customer, tackle it head on and clear the air before you put your message across. Don't be obsequious; you are unlikely to be respected for it. Display confidence, but stop short of cockiness. Don't be scared of a little cut and thrust—be tough enough to hold your corner—but avoid rudeness or being too dogmatic.

There are a few other points to keep in mind during a presentation:

- Don't knock the opposition or tell scurrilous tales about others in your industry, at least not until you know people well. Otherwise you may discover that your guests are bosom friends of the people you are attacking.

- Don't lose your temper if asked difficult questions. Handle objections convincingly and you will help your case. Anyone who buys something without asking searching questions may be a fool; a ruthless inquisition may be simply a search for knowledge as a prelude to buying. Anyway, if you can't handle questions you aren't properly briefed, are you?

- If you don't know something, say so. Offer to find out and do so.

- Don't make false promises. You don't have to be unduly pessimistic over such things as delivery dates but you should be realistic.

- If quoting some seemingly unbelievable statistic always state that you have double-checked it. Where necessary, elucidate by explaining that the doubling in sales was due to a warm spell of weather or whatever.

If it becomes clear during the presentation that the audience is getting impatient, sum up and shut up. And watch you don't trip over the steps as you leave the podium; it may be the only light relief of the day.

Finally, a word of caution on business presentations. Making them can be quite entertaining, especially if you enter the higher reaches with lavish sound and light shows. Don't get carried away by your entry into show business; be as objective as you would be about any other aspect of your organization's affairs.

8
Special occasions

This chapter discusses a few special functions where extra preparation or a different approach to a 'normal' public speech may be needed, but basically it simply reinforces the earlier point that you should always consider your audience when preparing a speech.

Family occasions

These should, in theory anyway, be relaxed, friendly affairs at which to speak.

The star guest at a **christening** is unlikely to understand any of your mellifluous meanderings, but if you are proposing a toast to a baby you should wish it a long and happy life, add a comment about its splendid parents and then propose the toast. Don't go on too long, otherwise the baby is likely to show its disapproval, even if everyone else is too polite to do so.

Moving up the age scale, the next family occasion at which a toast is necessary may be a **birthday**. As there will probably be more outside guests than relatives at birthday parties you should not make too many family references which may not be fully understood. Expect some ribaldry if the audience is young and/or has been at the champagne too long before you speak. A ghastly tradition has it that some self-opinionated old uncle is supposed to get up and reminisce about how the birthday boy or girl used to do this, that and the other as a small child, but the guest of honour won't thank you for doing so. So don't. You could however consider a tongue-in-cheek approach instead and say something like 'It is traditional on these occasions to embarrass the guest of honour by reminiscing about how Margaret used to roll about on the floor, chuckling, with a bottle and no clothes on; then as the aunts start just that sort of reminiscing, continue, 'but I'm not going to do that. What she did on holiday last year is her own affair.'

Moving further up the ages of man, **wedding** toasts seem to cause more anguish than any others. And so they should because you are most at risk from the latent tribal warfare which is only barely contained on some such occasions.

The theoretical running order at a wedding is that first an old acquaintance proposes a toast to the bride and groom. The groom replies on behalf of himself and his bride, pausing for applause as he says 'On behalf of my wife and I' for the first time. The groom then proposes a toast to the bridesmaids, to which the best man replies; he in turn proposes a toast to the parents. That's the theory, anyway, but it may be difficult to stop others jumping on to the bandwagon. The suffocating air of sentiment among older guests and the swill of booze among the younger ones mean that above all you should not prepare a long erudite speech because you will lose your audience. Worst offenders are usually those proposing the first toast to the bride and groom. Obviously if you are a groom responding to such a toast you must be sincere, and don't forget to mention your in-laws even if you usually only communicate with them through a solicitor.

Speeches at silver or golden **wedding anniversaries** should be given by old friends who know the couple well. It is entirely forgivable if they go on a shade too long.

Perhaps the most difficult speech you will have to make will be at the **funeral** of a relative or friend. Such occasions need great care and tact. In some places it is traditional to deliver a panegyric to the departed; these should be fairly brief. It may even be appropriate to tell jokes, or certainly anecdotes, at memorial services for well-known or particularly well-loved people—if it is done well.

Speeches will sometimes be called for at the gatherings which follow funerals; it may even be appropriate to mention that a memorial fund of some sort is to be started, but again great care is needed.

General occasions

Moving to general occasions, **retirement parties** or presentations sometimes cause a disproportionate amount of embarrassment, paradoxically because they involve people who work together every day and probably never see each other 'on stage' making a speech. Be as natural as possible and relate one or two things that have happened to the retiree over the years which, with luck, will amuse and at the same time show what a fine fellow he is. Bear in mind that young members of staff won't respond to a long anecdote involving someone who left the firm 20 years ago. It is usual to say that you hope the retiree 'will keep in touch' (although no-one is likely to remember him if he leaves more than six months before coming back) and as there is usually an awkward pause after the speeches, it helps if people crowd round to gasp at the engraved clock or whatever other horror the poor devil has to carry away.

If you are ever asked to propose a **vote of thanks**, then keep awake, listen to what the speaker says and in your speech just pick up one or, at the most, two points to show that you were paying attention. Don't go on too long and don't grind your own axes. Even if you disagree with every word, you should *not* go on the attack but instead should simply say something like 'I am sure we all found that unusual approach to the problem very thought-provoking.' Don't over-praise a speaker when he has clearly been totally out of touch with his audience, but do at least be polite.

When acting as toast-master or master of ceremonies and you have to **introduce** something, such as a cabaret, pitch up your voice to command attention and be enthusiastic enough to take the mood of the audience up a gear so that the shift from a rather dull dinner to an entertainer is not too sudden.

If you are making presentations at a **prizegiving** you will probably only be expected to say 'congratulations' to each of the prize winners as he collects his award. If more is expected, keep things short and relevant. If you have risen to the dizzy heights of presenting school prizes, assume you are addressing adults. Don't patronize the pupils by calling them kids or children; don't reminisce about what happened when you were a lad and avoid suggesting that all that is needed to cure the ills of the world is the return of national service. Don't ever think of trying to be 'with it' in your choice of words at a school prizegiving, unless you do so as a way of humorously confirming their view that you are on nodding terms with Methuselah.

(It occurs to me that you may think that I am being flippant about weddings, prizegivings and so on, but I am only trying to impress on you that you *must* consider the audience. If you simply orate platitudes or try to deliver a stirring message to mankind, well, you may like the sound of your voice, but your audience won't.)

If you are asked to **open a fête** then recognize that your audience won't want to stand about for too long, and remember that if you are in the open air you may need to pitch up compared with an indoor event in order to make an impact. And pay careful attention to the sound equipment. (Consider for a moment—have you *ever* been able to hear a word said by campaigners over car-mounted systems?) Plug the cause for which funds are being raised with a telling phrase or two and by referring to things to which the audience can relate—local comparison will produce a greater cash harvest than a lesson on macro-economics. After a short message, declare the fête, or whatever it is, open and then set off to buy your obligatory jar of jam.

When the purpose of your speech is **fund-raising** you need to work closely with the organizer so that you are on your feet at the most propitious moment; for example, people will donate more when they have had a glass or two of wine. Tell them what you are raising funds for and why. Incidentally, although you may be deeply involved with a particular project or charity, don't assume your audience is equally knowledgeable or enthusiastic but accept that you may have to sell your appeal. Never berate people.

This is one occasion when you should not read a speech. An 'appeal' must be just that, and preferably from the heart, so it should not be read. If there are tax advantages for your audience through covenants then say so and if you plan an auction to raise funds, approach one or two key supporters beforehand and ask them to start the ball rolling.

Annual general meetings (AGMs) really call for more skill on the part of the organizers than the speakers because the choice of venue, drinks and food (if any) and, above all, attention to the rulebook are as important as the words. If organizations are hard pushed to get anyone to attend an AGM, they should consider laying on something else to follow immediately afterwards, such as a film show. An AGM is one occasion when the speaker (who is likely to be the chairman) should not attempt to entertain or ad lib, but should simply concentrate on grinding through the business in hand.

If you are speaking at a **protest meeting** then you should not do so in isolation. You may be the spokesman for a group, but the planting of questions to be thrown at 'unfriendly' speakers or officials should be worked out in advance, as should the preparation of any banners to be waved and any stunts. Yes, stunts—in the weird media world in which we live, you may, perhaps reluctantly, have to resort to such things to attract attention. The key is an organizing group with broad interests. If all the members share a deep-seated but narrow view of the problem to be tackled, they are likely to be seen as bloody-minded bigots.

Elected officers, or candidates hoping to be so, won't need any advice from me about **political meetings**. If you are attending in the hope of asking questions, then position yourself where you can be seen and speak in a clear voice. Don't turn a question into a speech; the audience will react against you. The best practice for political meetings is to play charades with young children. It's the closest analogy I can draw, albeit rather unkind to children.

Whether we like it or not we live in a media world. Politicians plan their activities with television exposure in mind, and it behoves even the smallest organisations to promote themselves whenever possible by holding **press conferences**. If bee-keeping societies or motor clubs don't tell local newspapers what they are doing, they are missing opportunities to recruit new members.

But dealing with the press does need care. Don't waste journalists' time. Your message may be simple enough to be sent by letter instead of requiring their presence at a press conference. If you do invite journalists to a conference, don't give a formal speech but simply take them through your plans and then invite questions. If the news you have to announce is bad, then dress it up as best you can but do deliver it; if you try to conceal it you can bet you will be exposed.

Don't be scared of a little cut and thrust when you come to questions, provided tempers are not lost—a smooth bland press conference can be a very dull affair. If you are certain that a difficult question will come up, ask a friendly journalist to deliver it so that it is not quite as destructive as if fired by a more explosive character. If you are charged up, you may read more hostility into a question than is intended. If someone says, 'Is it true sales this month are the same as last year?', don't assume he is implying a poor performance. If the market is falling he may intend it as a compliment.

A few other points on questions:

- Don't put down a questioner as a clown; let other listeners draw their own conclusions. Always be polite.

- Don't let one person hog the questioning.

- If yours is a high-visibility area which makes national news then a handful of journalists may, under editorial pressure, be looking for exclusives and can blow trivia up into a major news story. Be cautious with off-the-cuff comments.

- If possible, handle radio and television interviews before or after the main conference. Other press correspondents will be irritated if they feel that they are being treated as second class.

The brightest journalists won't be satisfied with an open question session but will want their own private session with you later. Remember that competition among newspapers and magazines for sheer survival, coupled with aggressive interviewing techniques seen on television, may lead to young reporters quizzing you harder than you expected. This may strike you as rather harsh when all you are trying to do is announce that you are starting to raise funds for a new clubhouse, but don't let such an approach rile you. Just stick to the facts.

Never say that you 'expect' coverage, even if you've given journalists three free cups of coffee. And when, after all your efforts, a report appears with a mistake in it, don't charge round to the editor to complain. Write to him if it is a serious error, otherwise let it lie. The best way of preventing mistakes is to have a simple press release spelling our your plans, for example, where the clubhouse will be, how far you have got with planning permission, how much you hope to raise, and so on.

Two final points on the press. Check if the journalists are present whenever you are speaking and, if they are, guard against indiscretions you would not want to appear in print. And if you are actively seeking coverage, make sure journalists have a copy of the relevant section of your speech.

Debates

By including debates I am perhaps straying away from public speaking pure and simple, but if you do get involved then prepare as carefully as for a public speech. Above all you should be quite clear what the rules are.

Some of the best debates are heard at the Cambridge Union Society and I think it is worth quoting their forms of debate, which are printed on the back of handbills given to everyone attending so that, in theory, there is no confusion.

1   All speeches should be made as if speaking solely to the Chair. The President is usually referred to as either 'Mr President, Sir' or 'Madam President' as is

appropriate. Similarly, if someone other than the President is chairing the meeting, he or she is usually addressed as 'Mr Chairman' or 'Madam Chairman'. Members should stand up to speak, preferably by the despatch boxes, or else at their place in the House.

2 No member may slander or abuse any other member or guest. It is traditional to refer to other speakers as 'The honourable member'. 'The honourable member from . . . College' or in the case of Officers, ex-Officers and the Proposer and Opposer of a Motion as 'The honourable . . .'.

3 If the President interrupts the debate with his or her bell, all members save the one speaking at the despatch box should resume their seats.

4 Any member who wishes to apply for a paper speech should apply to the President on one of the forms available for such applications from the Office.

5 Any member who wishes to make a speech from the floor may either write to the President beforehand requesting such a speech, or indicate their willingness to speak during the debate by raising their hand when the President asks for speeches. If called, members should announce their name and college before beginning their speech. This is for the benefit of the Secretary and assists subsequent speakers who may wish to refer to points made in the speech later in the debate.

6 Cries such as 'Order', 'Hear, hear' and 'Shame' are permitted. Booing and hissing are not.

7 No speeches or interruptions may be made from the gallery.

8 The length of speeches is determined by the President. All speakers will be shown cards by the Secretary during the course of their speech showing how much of their time remains.

9   Members are entitled to interrupt proceedings on a point of order if they feel that the Laws or Standing Orders of the Society are being broken, and that the person chairing the meeting is not responding sufficiently. Such points have automatic priority over all other proceedings and should be introduced with the words 'On a point of order . . .'

10 Members are also entitled to offer points of information to the person speaking, although no speaker is *ever* under any obligation to give way to them. Points of information must be literally *points* of information and *not* small speeches. A member wishing to make such a point should stand up and remain standing until the person speaking indicates whether or not they wish to accept their point. If the speaker does not wish to give way the member wishing to interrupt *must sit down immediately*. Members sitting near the person wishing to make the point of information may cry 'Order' to draw the attention of the speaker to that person, *only* if it appears that the speaker has not seen them. Such points should be introduced with the words 'On a point of information . . .'

11 Members should always appreciate that visiting speakers are entitled to a quiet hearing and should not normally be heckled. Most of the speakers who visit the Union are very busy people who come as a favour to the Society, and should be treated accordingly.

12 Members may cast their vote by passing through the Ayes or Noes door at any time after the end of the second speech. They may vote only once, and members wishing the leave the Chamber without their vote being registered must leave through the centre doors.

I'm very much in favour of number 6! All perhaps a bit like the rules for square dancing and not really relevant to life away from university or other debating societies, but amusing none the less. My sole visit to speak in a union debate illustrated one of the points made elsewhere in the book: be clear about dress (see page 13). I was *told* it was evening dress but only the President and a sidekick, plus a lady speaker and I were so attired—the audience of 250 or so was in jeans. It almost looked as if the other speaker and I were to perform on *Come Dancing*.

9
Visual support

Visual aids would be inappropriate to support after-dinner speeches, but they often have a supporting role to play at talks, lectures and, of course, business presentations. But first, ask yourself if visuals are really necessary. They should not be used as crutches to prop up a poor presentation; polish up your words first and *then* decide whether to use visuals.

Visual aids can add interest and impact to a talk; as the cliché says, one picture is worth a thousand words. I wouldn't put it as high as a thousand, but it is certainly quite a lot. Even the lowering of lights to show films or slides may create excitement and/or intimacy, although the speaker will lose eye contact with his audience.

Here are a few general points to remember:

- *Always* concentrate on the words first before the visuals. Slides and charts will cost time and money, so be quite sure what you need *before* commissioning them. You don't have to stretch to elaborate typesetting for illustrations; a co-operative artist's free hand may be fine provided it is consistent.

- Tailor the lavishness of your visual aids to your audience and to the impression you hope to make. For a travel talk to a club by one of its members, a simple series of slides will be fine; a local or national company presenting to the same group should aim for a slightly more professional approach. Remember, the way you put your message across says something about your organization. If the slides are upside down or a projector fails, then it reflects adversely on you. Despite this advice, don't go absurdly over the top in your use of visuals. A massive sound and light show is perhaps not really necessary if you are just telling people about a new carpet-cleaning service.

- A poor visual aid is worse than none at all. The audience will stop listening to your words as it struggles to comprehend it.

- Don't cram too much information on to a slide or flipover but spread it over two or more.

- If you have to show columns of figures (and avoid them if you can), be consistent in their presentation. If years are shown across the top of the first illustration, don't put them vertically on the next. If you show a percentage for one statistic, don't put 6 out of 10 for the next.

- Write all words horizontally rather than vertically, even those on pie charts.

- Where several figures appear on a visual and one is central to your theme, circle or highlight it with a colour.

- Most audiences will include people who have forgotten their glasses, so use large visuals, and vet them from the back of the room. In particular, check if they are high enough for people at the back to see. (They rarely are.)

- Visuals must be honest. Graphs should not show a distorted view and facts must be accurate. Obviously you do not have to point out the adverse side of anything, but if you are caught trying to cheat and mislead people your credibility will disappear.

- Watch the question of confidentiality if visual aids of sensitive information are made by outside companies.

- If you need to refer to something twice, duplicate the illustration rather than shuffle back through a lot of flipover charts or rely on a projectionist to find a slide again. Cautious planners will have duplicate videos on hand in case one gets chewed up.

- First aid lectures apart, be wary of gory visuals— some people may faint.

- Don't overdo the use of pointers. There are retractable ones which clip in your pocket like a pen, or beams of light, or simply good old billiard cues; but first ask why you need to point at all. Is your illustration not clear enough in the first place?

- Check any equipment in advance. Never rely on a promise from a hotel that it will have what you need, even a piece of chalk: check.

- Rehearse with, or at the very least chat with, whoever will be working the lights so that he knows when you want them on, off or dimmed.

- Extraneous light must be kept out for some visual aids (slides, for example).

- Photographs of club officials or VIPs should be recent, not glamour shots taken years ago (otherwise they may receive a ribald welcome).

- When you have prepared all your visual aids, number them carefully to avoid confusion but *only* do so when everything is in place. Try not to number slides or charts 11A, 11B and so on.

Visuals must be tailored to the words. If you are talking about one figure while another is showing on the screen you will confuse your audience. If you are going to say 480, don't show 478. Unless total accuracy is needed, say for price increases or pay negotiations, use round figures. A figure of 1,100 will be easier to take in on a visual than 1,098 or 1,103. Give people time to digest what they see and fit the style of the visuals to your theme. For example, cartoons should not be used to illustrate a serious subject. (Cartoons need special care anyway; what some find amusing others will consider tiresome.)

Try not to mix visual aids. Bobbing about from flipovers

to video to slides may perplex your audience and will do nothing for the projectionist's peace of mind. One change is fine, say to introduce a film sequence, but avoid too many.

Now for a few specific points on various types of visual aids, starting with **slides**. And no, we don't want to see the ones you took on holiday, thanks all the same; holiday slides are eminently resistible unless the audience was present when they were taken. A local horticultural society's visit to a national show would perhaps be a suitable case for treatment.

Slides are the most widely used (and abused) visual aids, but to make the right impact with them, you need to remember a few basics.

- Avoid word slides where possible. Words should be heard, pictures should be seen. In particular, be sparing with word slides saying 'Objectives' or 'Good morning'.

- When you have no specific slide to illustrate a section of your talk, use a general picture or, better, the organization's logo or badge.

- Use a consistent style for slides if you are having them specially made. It will distract an audience if, for example, *the lettering keeps changing—as these words have probably distracted you.*

- If you do a lot of work with slides, a light box (an opaque flat surface with a variable light underneath) will be helpful because you can lay your slides on it to select and sort them. And when you've done so, don't forget to clean the slides—the slightest mark or speck of dust will show only too clearly on the screen.

- Use plastic mounts for slides rather than cardboard ones (which can buckle).

- Make sure you know how to use the remote control for a projector before your talk starts. If you fiddle with the controls, perhaps through nerves, you may inadvertently reveal your key message before you have built up to it in your speech.

- Put a blank slide at the start of a series so that you can switch on the projector to check it is working without anything showing on the screen. If you are really dedicated you can get special slides with graphics on them to help you focus the equipment.

If you are giving a talk or lecture using slides, you will probably have a fully written-out script, possibly with a second copy for the projectionist if you are not operating the equipment yourself. It is important that the script clearly shows the slide change points. There are many ways of doing this—for example, you could circle the words where you want a new slide, or put a line between the words. Do whatever makes you feel confident; it's not important what system you use. I break a script completely at a slide change point and write enough about the slide to tell me what should be on the screen, like this:

Make your notes for a speech on
SLIDE 16—CARD FOLDED TO GO IN POCKET
a piece of fairly stiff card which is folded so that it will go into an inside jacket pocket or handbag.

You soon get used to ignoring the capitals and reading 'through' them. This method makes it easy to sort slides into the correct order before a talk, while a projectionist would have to be fairly absent-minded to miss one of the change points.

Avoid cramming in so many slides that the audience misses the message you are trying to convey. 80 slides fit in a tray and you should try not to go above this figure. The growth of computer-generated graphic slides for business presentations means that complicated slides can now be prepared very rapidly and, with computers also used to operate multi-projectors, highly sophisticated presentations can result. But if you are ever told that you cannot react to circumstances and change a slide 'because it's in the computer', ease yourself out of the grip of technology next time and go back to a simpler system. You want people to remember your message, not the high-tech methods used to put it across.

Incidentally, give a little thought to when you are going to switch a projector off at the end of a presentation. The change in sound as the cooling fan stops may distract an audience; better still, get a silent projector.

Although slides are the most-used visual aids, **overhead projectors** (OHPs) will be ideal for many lectures. They are low cost and a speaker can face his audience all the time, although the system doesn't really work too well for large audiences. Although the transparencies used are easily made by writing on acetate sheets with a special felt-tip pen, it is worth the effort to make them neat and legible by using stencils for lettering. For a detailed lecture you can overlay one image on top of another to build up a story, although for elaborate illustrations it is probably better to prepare separate transparencies for each stage.

It is possible to obtain OHPs with attachments which allow a continuous roll of clear acetate to be used if you are planning to draw a lot of illustrations as you talk. If you have ready-prepared transparencies it is worth mounting them in card frames to protect them. Incidentally, an important advantage with an OHP is that you don't have to switch the lights off.

If you wish to show an audience such things as press cuttings and photographs without the trouble of making slides of them, then use an **episcope**, but bear in mind that you will need to put the lights off when doing so.

If you use **films or videos** as visual aids you are unlikely to be speaking while they are showing, but you must let the projectionist know exactly what you are going to say as an introduction (and don't ad lib) so that the films or videos start on cue. When you say 'now let's see the film,' a pause of only a few seconds will seem like an eternity.

Several sections of film to be shown one after the other may be spliced together with blank pieces between them so that the projector can be left running. Time the gap between each section, write suitable words to fit and rehearse the links carefully; resist the desire to speed up the linking sections during your presentation because this will cause awkward pauses. Make sure your microphone will be switched on at the appropriate moments.

At large venues you may find yourself projected on to a screen via a video system so that people at the back can see you. If so, guard against any distressing personal habits which might otherwise go unnoticed.

An elaborate slide-tape presentation which is to be shown several times could be put on to video and there may be other uses for video too. This is an area which is expanding rapidly and will continue to do so for a while yet. With interactive video disc systems it is possible for training purposes, and at exhibitions, to conduct two-way exchanges with answers to questions determining what is next shown on screens. If you think this is too complicated to use and won't become commonplace just look at the queues in front of bank cash dispensers which were equally startling when first introduced. If you have a clever process to demonstrate, a short video will do so better than any brochure or spoken words. But video is expensive and there are a lot of people willing to convince you that you want art for art's sake, so go into video with a level head.

For a smaller audience, **flipover charts** will be fine. Even large sheets of plain wallpaper will work, provided what is written or drawn on them is clear and legible. Put a blank sheet or a print of your organization's symbol over the first illustration so that the audience doesn't start reading until you want it to.

If you intend drawing on a chart during your talk, cheat a little beforehand and lightly pencil on the sheet what you want to illustrate, then boldly draw over the pencil marks with a felt tip during your presentation. You will be admired for your artistic, if not speaking, ability. With flipover charts, as with most other visual aids, use different colours to make the graphics clearer: for example, red to indicate dates of committee meetings, green to show social evenings, and a third colour giving film shows. Photographs rarely work well as flipovers— better to pin them around the walls for people to study later, perhaps.

Instead of flipping over sheets of paper, you can put your visuals on to cards which are then displayed on an easel. Plan them so that they will go under your arm, otherwise they may be awkward to carry.

For small groups a **portable presentation case** may be useful. There are various sorts available; some fold out like small easels, others are housed within a briefcase (which makes them easy to carry), but the basic principle is the same—they hold a series of clear plastic 'envelopes' into which you put cards, photographs and so on. The wallets are held on rings and you simply flip them over when you wish to move to the next visual. Practise with whatever type you use to ensure that you can set it up quickly; a client will not be impressed if your briefcase slides across the tables and knocks over his coffee during a business presentation.

Still for relatively small groups, **computers** may have their role to play. People are usually naïve enough to trust computers implicitly and if you are a businessman you may make a good impression with a micro-computer which is programmed to give an immediate answer to your customer's problems when he has given you one or two pieces of information. A printer will also leave him with a copy of your conclusions. But a computer is worth considering only if you learn how to use it properly; it will be conveying to people that yours is an alert, progressive organisation but you must remember the purpose of your presentation—don't concentrate on the wonders of the computer so much that you leave customers more concerned about buying one themselves than buying the product you were trying to sell them.

Moving away from high tech, don't neglect the beloved old **blackboard** as a visual aid; it worked well enough for us at school. As with flipover charts, lightly chalk in on the board things to be drawn later and then rub them out gently enough so that you can still see an outline to draw over. If you rub something out during a presentation, use a damp cloth which will avoid dreadful squeaks or your disappearance behind a cloud of chalk dust.

A hardened speaker becomes something of a survival expert and will carry such things as string, pins and sticky tape (the latter to tape pegs firmly on to easels).

More attractive than blackboards are **magnetic boards**. Things to be discussed can have magnetic pieces representing them cut to scale and these will stick on the board during a talk or lecture.

Or you could use a **white board** on which to write with special coloured markers. The boards are available double-sided so that you can swing a clean face into play when the first is full. If your budget will stretch even further, you can obtain such boards with built-in photocopies so that you can hand round A4 copies of what you have written. If you alert your audience to this facility it will mean that it can concentrate on your words without having to take notes.

You may consider **handing round** an object as a 'visual aid' during your talk. A 'Ming' vase which was made last week in Mablethorpe would certainly command attention if you were talking on false antiques. Handing this out needs care, however, because it can result in a certain amount of distraction and chatter as an object is passed along. Better to wait until the interval.

I once saw a crowd dive under their seats when a shot-putter hurled what they thought was a heavy object at it. In fact it was a rubber ball painted to look like a shot. It was hilarious at the time, but on reflection perhaps a bit risky; one or two people looked ready to pass out with fright.

And don't forget **lighting** and simple **room decoration** as visual aids. A little thought as to how a room should be lit and what emphasis should be put where can improve a talk or lecture, while a simple display of flowers or posters may brighten an otherwise dreary venue.

Finally, when using visual aids, do give audiences time to absorb them. Don't flick illustrations on and off. Put them on at the right time and, just as important, take them off at the right time too. An illustration should not be on display long after you have finished talking about it.

10
Rehearsing

When you have constructed your speech and prepared any memory aids, you need to consider what rehearsing to do before spellbinding your audience. As with so much in public speaking, it is a question of striking the right balance. You should run through your speech enough to highlight any clumsy links or phrases that may need to be changed, but you should not over-rehearse to the extent that all spontaneity slips away before your live performance.

I'm not an advocate of rehearsing in front of a mirror because this seems totally unnatural, but do take the trouble to say your speech aloud a time or two, and try to vary the pace so that it does not become monotonous. Stand up when you are rehearsing. You will tend to project more when on your feet, but the main advantage will be to see if you can actually read the notes you have prepared. If you wear glasses for close work, you may need to adjust the size of the writing on your notes so that you can read them at a glance, perhaps without glasses. A beautifully planned address may be ruined if your folder of notes is placed at the wrong height for you to read the words clearly.

Tape recording a rehearsal may alert you to distressing mannerisms, like 'you know' and so on, but the main problem with any rehearsal is lack of audience reaction, which is why timing can be slightly misleading because you can't gauge the length taken up by applause or laughter. You may consider that, if you are not attempting to be humorous, a dry run will give you a complete feel for what it will be like on the day because you will not be looking for an audience reaction. This is not entirely so because the fact that an audience is present *will* affect you; it may cause you to repeat a point or stress a particular section, or you may decide to delete something altogether.

One exception to the rule about avoiding too much rehearsal is where you have a fully written-out speech or lecture which is to be given with a lot of visual aids, such as slides. Here you will have to rehearse the presentation, preferably with the projectionist present, until you are able to read it without stumbling; almost inevitably you will have to edit it to make it flow. Even if you plan to read a speech right through, do remember to look up at frequent intervals to develop eye contact with your audience. Your rehearsal may show that some slides are on the screen for too short a time, if so either take them out or add a few more words so that the visuals can stay up longer.

If a speech or lecture has been assembled from material written by different people (as may happen to a chairman of an association who is delivering a report on several departments' work), the various sections should be 'tuned' to the deliverer's own style. In such a case the speaker should always ask himself if he *really* believes in what it is suggested that he should say; he may be less than persuasive if he doesn't.

Ask a long-suffering friend whose opinion you trust to listen to your rehearsal and tell you what message or messages he receives from your words. The friend needs to be fairly typical of the members of your expected audience for this to work properly. For example, if you are a boffin preparing to talk to a general audience, don't rehearse in front of a fellow boffin because he will be able to follow your abstruse references; find a less knowledge-able guinea pig.

While your long-suffering friend is sitting through your rehearsal, ask him to watch what you do with your hands. Some books on public speaking make much play of the importance of gestures, but I think such things should come naturally or not at all. While not planning deliberate hand movements, however, you should avoid any habits which are positively distracting; if you have any, try to control them. It is very off-putting to watch a speaker constantly fiddling with his glasses or putting his hands in his pockets then immediately taking them out again. Gestures which are carried to excess may even leave you open to ribbing. One speaker I saw wrung his hands so much that a voice asked, 'Are you cold?'

When a series of lectures or talks is to be given, it is important that someone sits in on all the rehearsals to listen for any inconsistencies. Even if it is too late to change any of the individual presentations, a chairman may be able to improve things by careful links between any jarring sections.

It may sound like cheating but if you have a key speech which you really want to hammer home to an important audience, you could consider a full-scale practice in front of a 'less important' audience in advance of your big day (in much the same way as plays tour the provinces before moving into the West End). The same applies to jokes because however hard you rehearse in private you need an audience to gauge the real reaction. Many comedians try out new material on sample audiences before using it in, say, a Royal Variety Show or television programme.

Whatever form your speech takes, sit back and have a final think after your final rehearsal. Have you held on to your message? Would your case be presented better if the running order was changed? Have you struck the right tone, or are you too hectoring, or not forceful enough? Now is the time to makes changes. Unhappily for audiences, not enough speakers go through this final analysis, either because they are just relieved to have cobbled something together or because they have run out of time.

At the same time as you review what you plan to say, decide if you are happy with the memory aids you intend to use. If you just can't get to grips with bullet points as notes, either write more detailed bullets or go back to reading the whole thing.

Although you will be unable to time applause or laughter during a rehearsal, it should at least give you an idea if your speech is *roughly* the right length; the most likely change you will need to make will be to shorten it. And do keep in mind all those earlier considerations about your audience. Yes, the secretary assured you that your audience would be a serious lot and, yes, your thoughts on the latest lunatic legislation to come out of Brussels are really terribly interesting. But don't you think 15 minutes would be better than the 25 you've got now (particularly if you find on the day that the wine has flowed fairly freely before you rise)?

It is often the practice to run sweepstakes on the length of speeches. A senior policeman, who shall remain nameless, once said as I was about to stand up: 'These sweeps are of course illegal . . . but please speak for exactly 13½ minutes.' Sweeps should not influence the length of your address as much as the thought that few professional entertainers can hold an audience for an hour, and even those that do may intersperse comic routines with songs. So why should a good after-dinner speaker think he is likely to hold an audience for half an hour? And, in turn, why should you even dream of going on for more that 15 minutes? Some excellent after-dinner speeches have lasted 40 minutes or so but, almost without exception, people have said afterwards 'What a pity he went on too long.'

The same concerns about timing apply to occasions other than dinners. A talk on jam-making or antique furniture to a broad audience should err on the side of brevity. If your audience is clearly expecting more when you finish, and the organizer is looking distraught because a meal or the next attraction is not yet ready, fill in by inviting questions.

As you use a rehearsal to break in a speech, use it also to try out new shoes. Squeaking ones may amuse some and distract others just as you are trying to command their attention. In addition, 'rehearse' new reading glasses and even false teeth. To test the latter, try saying 'Stress is a major source of suffering in single Siamese cats.' If in doubt, go back to your dentist.

Audiences can be very cruel.

Business functions

It may not be vital to pay much attention to rehearsing a short speech to a small social group but every business presentation should have a rehearsal, however brief. The first may just be a 'stagger-through' to see if the words are right and the correct visuals are available. Time the various sections to provide a rough estimate of the overall length and include the boss in this rehearsal. Don't let him say: 'Oh, I'll just say a few words at this point about the product,' otherwise come the day and he'll launch into a full product reveal, wrecking the running order. He should go through his words like everyone else.

After this rehearsal think about the overall impact. Have you put your message across? Rejig words and/or visuals if necessary and don't be afraid to drop any particular slide or passage in the script if it obviously is not working.

Try to hold a full rehearsal in the actual meeting place. Make an accurate timing of this dry run, allowing for introductions, prizegiving ceremonies, and so on and rehearse how speakers will get on and off stage without bumping into each other. If they have a long walk to a podium they should start moving up as they are being introduced to avoid an uneasy pause; they should then try to arrive with apparent confidence, no matter how nervous they may be.

If you are making your presentation to several audiences of different sizes, you should programme your introduction sequence accordingly. If your presentation starts with a computer-controlled sequence of slides and music to give people time to sit down, and this is prepared for a large audience, it will be too long for a smaller group and will keep churning away long after they have sat down, destroying the mood. The answer is to start the sequence and let it run for a while before calling people in.

After your full rehearsal, consider again the overall impact and above all the time you have taken and if in doubt *shorten*. Axe any waffle. Remember that the brightest people may have the shortest attention span.

11
Nerves

Nerves cause more alarm among those people invited to speak than any other single factor and fear certainly leads many people to refuse opportunities to speak. It is a great pity because nerves *can* be kept in check.

This chapter was originally called 'Conquering nerves' but that is almost impossible; in fact, total control of nerves may be undesirable because a certain amount of nervousness can add sparkle to a speech. And take comfort—the terror, the sweaty palms, the dry lips, the urge to run to the lavatory are all quite natural. Honestly. Nervous tension is a perfectly normal reaction to any strong emotion and is something of a throwback to uncivilized life thousands of years ago (slightly less time if you are speaking at a rugby dinner) when meeting an adversary meant that you had to put the maximum effort into either fighting or running away. Emotion starts adrenalin chasing about your body, your heart rate increases, your blood pressure rises and sweat glands in the skin work overtime to carry away the excess heat produced. But hold on—don't put the book down yet. All that hyperaction is perfectly normal and is just your body getting ready to perform at maximum efficiency. And remember that it's not just confined to public speaking—actors, sportsmen and many others go through exactly the same process before performing.

Those are the scientific reasons (using scientific in the loosest sense of the word, I hasten to add) for your terror, but before you refuse an invitation to speak, it's worth trying to identify the causes of your particular metabolic madness.

- Inexperienced? Never spoken before? Well, recognize that you really should start some time; in a world which depends so much on communication it is silly to remain silent.

- You don't know anything about the subject? Then don't speak. (Would that more speakers would follow this advice.)

- You've been asked to propose a toast or vote of thanks and it all seems too important for humble old you? This should be the least of your worries. A toast is the easiest speech of all to make, particularly if it is not preceded by a long build-up, while a vote of thanks simply means that you are acting as a spokesman for the rest of the audience in saying 'thank you'. The biggest snag with the latter is that you may be the only member of the audience who has to stay awake while a speaker drones on.

The main reason for being inclined to refuse an invitation to speak is likely to be the fear of making a fool of yourself. Go back to an earlier point—do you know something about the subject? If you do then you needn't make a fool of yourself. So accept.

I recognize that you may be a naturally timid person who simply doesn't want the hassle of screwing yourself up to speak in public. But before you finally put this book down just think of some of the advantages.

You will be able to present your case better if you are lobbying for or against something (such as an airport on your allotment) or trying to raise funds for a favourite charity. You will be able to communicate better with others and, for instance, pass on enthusiasm for your hobby. Confidence in speaking may even help you to a better job because you will perform better at interviews. The benefits are endless. You could even entertain people with a witty after-dinner speech—and don't let anyone tell you it isn't rewarding to get warm applause after a speech which has gone down well. It is. Go to work on an ego.

And just for a moment, stop thinking of yourself—consider the audience instead. I don't know about you, but if speakers get it all wrong I want to crawl under the table with embarrassment for them. Yes, an audience can get nervous too, either if you gabble away from the start or, worse, if they think you are going to drone on for so long that the bar will be closed. People will enjoy themselves much more if they sense that you know what you are doing and are confident.

Having considered why you suffer with nerves and the benefits of controlling them, how can you exert that control?

First, vow not to use drugs or alcohol to steady your nerves. I've read an article in a magazine which should know better suggesting that the majority of top public speakers take beta-blockers. Nonsense. They don't.

If you take drugs regularly for a specific complaint then you will obviously continue to do so while speaking, otherwise don't be tempted by even a tranquillizer; be wary too of taking simple medicaments without a doctor's advice—I heard one horrendous speech which went wrong simply because a glass of wine had reacted with something and caused very strange speech patterns in a speaker. In fact, everyone should be wary of taking alcohol when speaking. One glass may be fine, but take two and the microphone will magnify the oh-so-small, but oh-so-noticeable, slur to your words.

So no drugs or alcohol. Let's try self-analysis instead. Can you talk to a group of friends at a coffee morning or cocktail party? Of course you can. Then you can also talk to a larger audience. A coffee morning isn't public enough to be a fair comparison? Then go and ask questions at a political meeting or at a local lecture. Get used to the sound of your own voice raised in public (not too stridently, though). Even buying something at an auction will give you practice because you will have to shout out your name to the auctioneer. I remember feeling very nervous the first time I did that, now I buy what my family considers the most appalling junk with total aplomb.

Reading aloud, either to yourself or to a masochistic friend may help to develop your technique and put expression into your voice—although do choose an author who uses simple words and short sentences with no jargon. You could even go on a professional training course to improve your speaking skills, but be careful. These courses have a tendency to turn everyone out as if they've been cast in the same mould, perhaps because they are aimed mainly at businessmen facing similar situations. Also, as you get to know the others on your particular course you will gain confidence in front of them and then be scared all over again when you face a new audience.

Now that so many people have home video equipment it may be simpler, and certainly cheaper, for a group of friends, perhaps from the same society, to run their own DIY training course. Several videos are available which illustrate the key points to keep in mind and, after watching one, individuals could be asked to stand up and give a two-minute speech to the rest of the group on a subject they have prepared beforehand. It is even better if these speeches can be filmed and played back on a TV screen while the group is encouraged to be mercilessly critical of one another. After their two-minute prepared speeches, participants could be asked to ad lib for a minute or so on a subject pulled out of a hat. Having to speak off the cuff on, say, wheel clamps and their place in a welfare state should give you so much to think about that you will forget your nerves.

You will have gathered by now that a key factor in successful speaking is preparation and then practice. I suspect that great speakers must be born with an acute sense of timing and 'feel' but anyone can improve with practice and certainly you will be able to control your nervous tension with proper preparation. So, if there is the remotest chance that you will be asked to make a brief speech, do a little preparation. You don't think the breathless addresses from Oscar winners, thanking their agents and directors and praising motherhood and apple pies, are unrehearsed, do you?

And we have agreed that you will try to avoid speaking unless you know what you are talking about, haven't we? Confidence in your knowledge of the subject will help you to relax and control your nerves, but don't relax so much that you send your audience to sleep—a point which boffins or the very knowledgeable need to watch when addressing less erudite audiences.

To some extent your subject matter may affect your nervous tension. If you are raising an unpopular topic you may anticipate the going getting rough. As an extreme example, I wouldn't relish giving a speech in defence of cigarette smoking to many audiences nowadays. I suppose the only hope would be to concentrate on the 'freedom of choice' angle, but even then I think I'd find a train to catch before there was time for any questions.

Now let me digress briefly to consider those who stutter or stammer. I do not have the knowledge or impertinence to offer a cure and anyway sufferers with the problem will no doubt have had all the skilled advice they need. But, if it is any consolation to stutterers and stammerers, out of my personal 'top ten' of speeches I've really enjoyed, two were given by speakers with speech impediments— speakers who had the confidence to make the problem work *for* them in making an impact.

Now back to the main body of my sermon. If you have accepted an invitation to speak, recognize that there comes a time to stop preparing and worrying. You've done all you can, so why get ulcers? Regard the occasion as something to be proud of, not nervous about; *you* have been chosen to speak, not someone else. Many people kid themselves that they could write a book; few believe that they could make a speech, so most of the audience would be equally nervous in your shoes and therefore you will have plenty of sympathy from the start. I've listened to over a thousand speeches or lectures and I've only heard one person dry up and that was because of mixing alcohol and medicine.

Your nerves may still be there when you get to your feet, of course, but you will be too busy to worry about them unless you go adrift, and even then a mistake will make you seem more human. In fact, if you make a mistake in front of an audience which knows you and someone gently heckles you, he may actually help you to relax and perform better.

Incidentally, even if you have been nervous when making a speech or giving a lecture, you will be less so when answering questions afterwards because your brain will be too busy working out your replies. If you don't know an answer, say so. Don't waffle.

One final thought—public speaking isn't the end of the world. I've never actually heard anyone's knees knock with fright and, apart from occasional politicians, who don't need our sympathy, no-one actually gets physically hurt when public speaking!

12
Before you speak

Your preparation to speak should start even before you leave home on the great day. Is your hair tidy? Although you should be yourself, you may distract an audience if you look like a scarecrow, unless of course you are speaking on crop protection or conservation when it might be an advantage to appear slightly unkempt.

Be over- rather than under-dressed—as a speaker you will to some extent be 'on stage'. Having received wrong instructions and spoken in flannels at an evening dress affair and in a monkey suit when the rest were in casual clothes, believe me, the latter is best. If you are wrong-footed in either direction you could make some lighthearted reference to it in your speech: 'I know your treasurer is always pleading for more funds, but I didn't think he'd extracted so much money from you that I'd be the only one here tonight able to afford evening dress.'

For informal functions, aim to be slightly more formally dressed than the majority, say in a suit while most are in more casual clothes, although if you are talking about sheep dog training presumably you could get away with the sort of tweeds which look as if they are made from chunky marmalade and, of course, if you take a dog along too the audience will forgive anything you do.

Your clothing should be comfortable without anything tight around the neck. This is one area where women are at a mild disadvantage. Their appearance is likely to be more critically examined than men's, who are able to shelter behind their anonymous penguin suits at formal functions. Both sexes should avoid an overt display of jangling jewellery, unless they want to look as if they are about to start reading palms.

Remember to take your notes with you when you leave home. Pencil on the top any points to query when you arrive; for example, do you need to refer to a 'council' or a 'committee'? For some functions you may need money for cloakroom tips or raffles. A freshening sachet as supplied with airline meals is worth using shortly before you speak.

Leave home in ample time to reach the venue without being rushed. You will not be at your best if you've sweated through traffic jams to arrive just as your name is being announced.

Take a book with you in case you arrive far too early and have travelled by car. It is better to sit in it quietly reading rather than get under the feet of the organizers or spend a long time chatting with officials before the start. Of course, you can use the time to browse through your notes again, but a book or magazine may calm you more.

On arrival, check the room in which you will be speaking as soon as possible. If you foresee any problems—the room is so big that the audience should be shepherded to the front, or it is too hot or too cold—tactfully mention them to the organizers when you meet. Note 'tactfully'. Organizers will not relish neurotic busybodies trying to change everything, but they may welcome sensible suggestions learned by you from bitter experience as a speaker. Will the audience be able to see you? Maybe you will be speaking in an informal area, perhaps while people are buying coffee or cocktails. If so, find a chair or table to stand on because the people will concentrate more than if they are straining to see you across the heads of fellow guests.

Is the lectern at the right height for you? If necessary stand on a box because you will look faintly ludicrous if you can only peer over the top of the lectern. Check also that the height of the table or lectern on which your notes will be resting is correct for your eyesight.

You may be able to do little about the seating arrangements except tactfully point out to the organizer anything which seems really hopeless. Never have your back to anyone when speaking. Preferably have your back

to a wall and be seated roughly at the centre of one wall so
that you have the best eye contact with your audience.
The worst situation for a speaker is where a top table faces
an empty dance floor with tables of guests at either side—
most disconcerting. Incidentally, sometimes guests are
unavoidably placed in an annex or even in another room
altogether with an extension speaker. If so, make some
reference to their plight during your speech, perhaps
something along the lines of: 'We've enjoyed our caviar
here in the main hall, I hope you enjoyed your fish and
chips in the poor peoples' section.'

Organizers should not place speakers in front of
windows: the light will distract an audience and may give
a speaker an unwarranted halo. If you find yourself in this
position when speaking during daylight hours, ask for the
curtains to be drawn behind you (provided there is
enough light from other windows) otherwise a cheery
window cleaner with his chamois leather or a pretty girl
strolling by in the street will prove far more riveting to the
audience than your words.

Remember you will need a light on a lectern; cautious
speakers will also have a torch near to hand. If you are
sitting at a table on a stage then a cloth over it and down to
the floor is desirable.

All the above considerations assume that you use your
eyes when you arrive at a venue. Now use your ears. Is
the air conditioning noisy? Is there a public address
system? Is it playing muzak? Ask for them to be turned off
before you speak. Even the hum of a refrigerator in a bar at
the back of a room can distract. And if you spot a phone in
the function room ask if it has been disconnected or, at
least, if the operator has been told not to put calls through.
If you don't do this, the one thing you can be certain about
is that it will ring at a key moment in your speech.
Obviously, as a nervous speaker approaching your first
big moment, you will not wish to start over-organizing,
but if intrusive noise does spoil your speech, *you* will be
the one to suffer so make a mild fuss in advance if you feel
it will reduce the risk.

As you walk through an empty venue with an organizer
before a function starts, you will be able to hear each other

clearly and you may therefore be inclined to do without a microphone but if in doubt, *use one*. The rustle of movement from any audience and the chatter from ruder ones when people are speaking make this advice essential. If you have to struggle to make yourself heard it will put a strain on you and may kill the flow of your delivery. If you have a microphone and find you don't need it, you can always push it to one side. Ideally, you should try out microphones beforehand but if this isn't possible then at least study how earlier speakers get on with the equipment. If you are following other speakers check how tall they are. This will act as a guide to whether you will need to adjust the height of the microphone.

Even the sight of a technician present during a function doesn't mean that you can relax your vigilance about microphones. His presence may simply mean that the equipment is so unreliable that running repairs are usually necessary. He may, however, at least be able to stop the microphone howl which causes audiences so much hilarity and is often caused by the poor placing of speakers in relation to microphones.

If the public address system continually gives trouble while you are speaking, push the microphone aside and carry on without it, if necessary moving in among your audience to make yourself heard.

Many speakers swear by microphones worn on a cord around the neck because their voice will still be picked up if they move their head from side to side. Mikes clipped to a jacket collar can come adrift and both these and neck mikes do take a little getting used to. For most occasions a stand-mounted microphone is probably the best, preferably a short stand placed on a table; having to speak at a floor-standing microphone makes you look as if you are about to burst into song. As a last resort you can use a hand-held mike, but this does tie up one hand, thus restricting your gestures and making it more awkward to cope with notes.

Whatever microphone you use, guard against off-the-cuff comments when the equipment may be live. If you say to the chairman 'They were a dim lot' as you sit down and it booms out over the address system, it could bring any applause to an abrupt halt.

As well as checking the venue and microphone, try to find the answers to the pencilled points on the top of your notes and do check people's names. If you are planning to refer to or rib someone, it is worth mentioning it to the organizer. It would be in bad taste to mention someone who has recently been declared bankrupt or had a serious illness, for example.

As well as checking what you are going to say about others, try to find out what they in turn plan to say about you in their introduction. A club member may have assembled a long list of your outstanding achievements, but for heaven's sake persuade him to cut it down to just enough key points to establish your right to be addressing the audience. At a more mundane level, if you are expecting a lift back to the station establish from whom.

Make yourself known to the master of ceremonies or toast-master beforehand to check how they propose to introduce you. One MC asked me if I would signal when I was within a couple of minutes of the end of a speech to a very distinguished gathering. Helpfully I did so and to my surprise was nearly bundled off the stage by the stripper who was due to follow me. Memories are made of this.

Enquire if there are any presentations or raffles which are likely to disrupt the flow of speeches and, if necessary, gently ask if the running order can be changed. If fund-raising raffles follow a lunch then the speaker coming later may find his audience drifting away (although if there is plenty of time, running a prizegiving or whatever before the speaker may put the audience in a good mood).

A speaker will often be invited into a VIP area for drinks with senior officials. It would be discourteous not to join them, but don't succumb to too many offers for all the obvious reasons.

If you are at a meeting to put across a message and a television crew is there, make sure it knows which is your key section and offer to do a separate interview if it will help your cause. The same goes for radio.

Try not to be thrown off balance by an unforeseen

happening which affects what you planned to say. If the chairman is ill and the president is taking over his duties, go through your notes deleting the references to Fred and substituting ones to Arthur. The revisions may be more substantial if a major event occurs, such as the resignation of a key politician or a devalution or a council changing its mind about a bypass. You will have to use your judgement at such times but just recognize that, however rigidly you have prepared, you may have to modify your notes under certain circumstances. If something changes just before a business presentation and your visuals are already locked into the computer then at least ad lib a comment to explain the changed circumstances.

Have a supply of water available in case you dry up while speaking; a carafe is better than a jug because there is less landing space for flies. The water should not be too iced as this can have an adverse effect on your throat.

Still before the function has begun, brush your clothes, switch off the alarm on your wrist watch and . . . well, do any other small things you may think of. You may develop a pattern of behaviour before speaking that is really due to nerves, but a routine helps to soothe them.

When the event has started, but still before your oration, there may be a break before any speeches. If not, it is still worth nipping out around coffee time if it is a dinner. (Tell your neighbour whether you want black or white.) Grab a breath of fresh air if you have been sitting in a stuffy smoky atmosphere during a meal. Use your freshening sachet or better still, if you are in a hotel and have a room booked, slip up and have a quick wash and clean your teeth. This will liven you up.

Back at the table, clean your glasses if you wear them and empty your pockets of bulky items because your clothes will look smarter. By this stage you should have a clear idea of the mood of the audience, which at dinner may depend on how freely the wine has flowed—too much and they may have become 'brittle' and mildly hostile. If they are throwing bread rolls by this time, you will be wise to cut any whimsical references to Beatrix Potter from your speech.

You may not be making an after-dinner speech but,

whatever the occasion, the moral is to keep the audience in mind at all times. With experience you will 'feel' the atmosphere in a room and this will guide you on whether, for example, to delete long, complicated anecdotes; you should certainly do so if the atmosphere feels at all cold or staid.

Listen to any other speakers while you are waiting to perform. Even if they are dull they may say something which affects what you plan to say. It is a bit rude to sit writing down their jokes (although this often happens) but you should listen to the points they make because you may want to delete the same ones in your speech, or rebut them, or simply add 'As Sarah said . . .' before supporting the same view. As well as listening to what is said, listen for what is *not* said. If no-one else has thanked the organizer for an excellent event then do so in your speech; it may be the only round of applause you will earn.

If you are a supporting speaker for a bigger 'star', tailor your notes accordingly. The audience certainly won't want you to drone on. Be prepared to cut too if you stand at the end of a long line of speakers. Some organizers seem to vie over the numbers of speakers they field, and such marathons often ask too much of audiences. Similarly, if things are running late, cut if necessary and say early in your address that you plan to end by a certain time.

With luck, your organizer will have cleared the decks ready for any speeches and at a dinner staff will have cleared away coffee cups. In fact it is worth hinting that you will not be prepared to speak if staff are still wandering in and out or collecting drinks bills during speeches. (It has been known.) This sounds pernickety but an audience should be ready to listen before you begin and it won't be if it is distracted. It only needs a couple of people whispering at the back of a room to wreck your carefully thought-out speech.

Place yourself near to the front of the room before you are introduced if you are to speak on a stage otherwise you may arrive to the chilling sound of your own footsteps. Don't, however, slink on stage as if you are ashamed of what you are going to say.

When your time comes (the deathly phrase is not entirely inappropriate) put out any cigarettes or cigars. Never smoke while speaking. Yes, I know some comedians use cigarettes as props for their acts and a cigarette may soothe your nerves, but it won't do your voice much good and you will look clumsy if you are also holding notes.

If you happen to follow a brilliant speaker, try not to be put off. Perhaps start with 'I've heard many brilliant speeches in my time, but that was the best' and then carry on exactly as planned.

Be warned that some associations have friendly, but off-putting, traditions which may affect you as you are about to speak. Speakers may be introduced with a medley of tunes relevant to their professions, played by a military band. It has been known for speakers' names to be greeted with a thunder flash and a deliberately over-elaborate trumpet fanfare. Your introduction to the noble art is likely to be less hectic but as you are about to be introduced do *switch on*. If you have had a rough day and the world seems against you, well that is your problem—the audience won't want to know. It is there to be entertained or informed, so forget everything else and concentrate on that. Change up a gear when you are ready to perform and *concentrate*. No-one said it would be easy but, if you've followed the advice so far, you've done all the preparation you can.

Now stand and deliver.

13
Delivery

Delivery is what public speaking is all about; no matter how thorough your preparations, you still have to put a speech across properly.

I don't plan to lay down too many hard and fast rules about delivery but there is one important law: be yourself. Be as natural as possible in all you do. You are on show in front of an audience so although you should not slouch, nor should you stand as if you are about to drill a squad of guardsmen.

Being yourself means being sincere, *genuinely* sincere. (You should not look as if you have had lessons in sincerity.) An audience will quickly detect someone who is either lying or clearly hasn't much belief in what he is saying.

Use your normal voice. Don't try to alter the pitch even if your voice is normally high and squeaky—straining to change it may make things worse—and if it reverts to its normal pitch in the middle of a key passage, it will amuse your audience no matter how serious your message.

You are more likely to speak naturally if you are using bullet points rather than a fully written-out speech because you will use spontaneous phrases rather than carefully honed words which may not really be 'you'; over-polishing can make things sound artificial. The best way to avoid running out of breath is to shun long sentences; short ones with well-timed pauses between them will be more effective.

If your family or friends rib you for putting on a 'posh' voice on the phone, take care not to do this while speaking. Apart from the fact that you won't sound natural, a too-formal or plummy accent is actually a disadvantage when public speaking. If you drop the occasional aitch, don't waste time trying to pick it up; you will only draw further attention to your slip and may even tack it back on to the wrong word. Never drop aitches deliberately or 'talk common' to show that you are one of the lads because this will be seen as offensively patronizing.

An accent or dialect may be an asset when speaking. A French person speaking English with an accent can be devastatingly erotic, while a strong regional accent can add character to a speech provided it is understood. Avoid phrases which don't travel—a saying in common use in Cornwall could be incomprehensible in Clapham, or vice versa.

In being yourself, try not to orate other than as a direct parody of the genre. Aim to be clear, not loud. Aim at the back of the room and try not to talk out of the side of your mouth; it will look underhand or as if you are a ventriloquist.

A successful speech relies on its **content**. If you have nothing to say, why on earth are you on your feet? Your content should be well fixed in your mind whatever form of notes you are using. Don't apologize for any lack of speaking experience. You may have been over-praised in the introduction and, if so, it is worth gently deflating the praise by a little self-mockery. If you don't do this or, worse, seem to preen at the words, your audience will sense that you are a self-satisfied ass. Equally, you should not scatter undeserved praise around in your speech; if the meal was lousy, better not to refer to it than praise it.

Is your subject likely to be boring? If so, you may risk warning your audience, taking care to explain *why* the subject is dry but, equally, why it is so important. For example: 'I'm going to be throwing a lot of apparently boring figures at you as we look at the next five years. Please consider them carefully because they show that if we don't do something our club will be bankrupt well before the five years are up. Yes, bankrupt.'

If you get lost during your speech, recapping on the

points you have made so far may bring you back on track. A highly charged subject where precision in the choice of words is vital (such as a planning matter or industrial relations negotiation) may require you to read a key piece; better to seem a little formal during such a section than to be misunderstood or misquoted later.

Don't forget to build in signposts during your speech so that you carry your audience with you—'Having considered apples, now let us look at pears.' Preface occasional paragraphs with 'Mr Chairman, what we must do is . . .' or 'Ladies and gentlemen, I think it is important to remember . . .' These will add a touch of courtesy to your speech and at the same time act as mild break points, worth using at the start of a key section for example.

Avoid making asides to the chairman or anyone on the top table while you are speaking. It is discourteous and treats part of the audience as outsiders, which will be resented.

Finally, do have a good finish. Too many speakers pay great attention to their introduction and then tail away. It is better to do the reverse and concentrate on the finish because that will be the part people remember longest. Summarize what you have been saying and, if you are calling for action, stress *exactly* what you want to happen. Don't leave people thinking 'Yes, what a shocking problem' without knowing what they can do to correct it.

The **flavour** of a speech is less tangible than the content, but in your earlier planning you should have given some thought to the tone you hope to project. Are you trying to entertain, convince, motivate, or what? Pitch your approach and tone accordingly. You need to speak with enough conviction to control your audience without making authority sound like superiority. Don't be too intense. If you stare at your audience wild-eyed and thump the table too often in your attempts to convince them of the benefits of macrobiotic food, guests may simply conclude that you are deranged and switch off to your message.

Occasionally, very occasionally, a judicious loss of temper will add impact to a speech, but generally it is better to keep calm and adopt a gentle approach. Some of our more extreme political figures realize this and are perhaps at their most dangerous when they are being sweetness and tolerance personified on radio and television question panels.

In being yourself, don't be afraid of a bit of sentiment or even an occasional tear if it is an emotional subject about which you feel strongly. But such human touches must be spontaneous. For a similar reason you should avoid deliberately rehearsed 'mistakes', perhaps in an attempt to get a laugh, because they invariably sound false. As an example, a spontaneously lighthearted comment after someone has dropped a plate will amuse, but don't ask for plates to be dropped deliberately because you will be waiting for it to happen and your response will sound forced.

Be careful with your use of first names. As a general rule it is more relaxed and friendly to talk about Jack Smith than Mr Smith in a speech (and I wish organizers would always put first names on menus and place cards), but don't go overboard. If you are speaking in front of a high sheriff, it could be a bit tactless to call him 'Alf'; and don't let us down by asking where he has left his bow and arrows, will you?

Don't attempt to maintain an even pace throughout your speech because you won't be able to do it. In any case, an even delivery can be monotonous if understated and exhausting if over-enthusiastic. Be enthusiastic, but don't gush. If your normal speech is slow and deliberate, perhaps you could speed up a shade. The audience hears much faster than you can speak because the endings of some sentences are predictable and the audience will have reached them before you have said them; they may use the time lag to let their minds wander. The use of pauses is a delicate area—you need them as punctuation, but they must be so timed that you keep the audience concentrating.

Once familiar with the outline of your speech, be careful not to digress or elaborate on one point too much as this may mar the rhythm and pace of the whole.

With experience, you will 'feel' the vibes from an audience and sense how your speech is being received.

The initial mood of an audience, of course, will be beyond your control. If listeners have had a a heavy day, followed by a large meal, they may be nearly asleep. It simply means that you will have to work that much harder to get a reaction from them.

Timing is even more important than flavour and here we come back to those pauses, the most important of which is right at the start of your speech. As you are introduced, don't leap up and start gabbling away immediately. Instead, pause just long enough for the audience to look at you and for you to establish your presence before speaking, but not so long that someone shouts 'Get on with it.'

Never apologize for lack of time in preparing a speech; that is your problem not the audience's. Absorbed though you may be with your words, you must have an awareness of real time while you are speaking. At a carefully planned series of lectures you may cause chaos if you promise to speak for 45 minutes and stop after 10, but at a dinner where the meal has overrun be prepared to shorten your speech, particularly if dancing is to follow. The emphasis on timing is one of the reasons why in your planning you should have sorted your information into an order of importance and then marked your notes, perhaps with a colour code, so that you know what to delete (see page 34).

Give your audience time to digest statistics before moving on to the next point. If the noise level starts to rise as you are speaking, however, then you have lost the audience; shut up rather than try to shut it up. If you insist on ploughing on you will get perhaps the most insulting 'applause' of all—ironically loud clapping and ribald shouts of 'more'. Conversely, if your speech is going well *do not* be tempted to extend it; quit while you are ahead.

On some occasions it will be useful to have preplanned signals so that, for example, someone at the back can let you know that a film has arrived or the bar is ready to open and you can draw to a close. Next time you are at a dinner try to spot what the head waiter's signal is to staff to start them clearing a course away. Similarly, use of a particular phrase or gesture means that you plan to finish in five minutes, so that bar staff can be alerted or papers got ready to be handed out.

Take care about overt signals to the audience itself. 'My last point is . . .' will alert some that an end to their agony is near, but it may also encourage others to nip out to be first for the toilet or the hot pies, and the exodus will disrupt your speech. Worst sin of all for a speaker is to say 'Finally, ladies and gentlemen . . .' and then drone on for several more minutes. It is quite infair to raise false hopes in your audience.

If you are being yourself you will probably make spontaneous **gestures** while you are speaking. They certainly add warmth to an address but resist the temptation to create them deliberately, never over-act and never wag your finger at an audience as if you are admonishing it.

There are no hard and fast rules about **stance and posture**. Try to stand naturally. Of course, if you rock from side to side while speaking you may put your audience to sleep; it works with babies. If you are using notes, don't be furtive about them. Audiences are used to seeing VIPs read speeches on television (often very badly), so they will not be surprised that you use notes too.

The previous points in this chapter assume that all is going well with your speech but, of course, you may occasionally have problems.

These may come early in a speech if there are a lot of latecomers. Welcome them to show that you are aware of their arrival (your audience will be) and, if appropriate, quickly sum up where you are.

Don't fall into the trap of asking if people can hear at the back. Someone is likely to say 'Yes, but I'll gladly change places with someone who can't.' Better to have a friend at the back primed to signal if he can hear.

Try not to be thrown out of your stride by a clanger. The chill in the room if something goes wrong and embarrasses the audience will be unsettling but, when appropriate, you should keep going. (Obviously if someone is taken ill, you may have to break off.) If you inadvertently use a word or phrase which has an unfortunate double meaning, be careful that in correcting the mistake you don't actually make it worse. Better to grin along with the audience and carry on.

You may need ad-libbing powers if you ask your audience questions, however rhetorical. In answer to what should we do about the Birth Control Bill, some wag may shout 'Pay it'!

At the intrusion of a police siren the comment 'Just let me make this point before they take me away . . .' will raise smiles, however unfunny it may look in print.

Perhaps the worst time for ad libbing is when you are unexpectedly asked to say a few words at the last minute. If there is the remotest chance of this happening give a little thought to it before the function, otherwise **be brief**. Never attempt a long speech without proper preparation.

Whatever the occasion and however you are received, once you are on your feet **concentrate**. It is possible to be in full cry and still find your mind wandering, but that means that you are either coasting through your words through over-familiarity, or you are altogether too relaxed and heading for a fall. And consider, if you can't concentrate when you are *saying* the words, how on earth is your audience expected to when it is trapped into *listening* to them?

Before you get on your feet you should know what will happen at the end of your stint. Are you to propose a toast, hand the meeting back to the chairman, or introduce another lecturer? Be clear in advance so that there isn't an anti-climactic pause. If you have delayed points to put across in a speech, perhaps as part of a lobbying campaign or at a press conference, then, of course, have copies available for distribution.

It is common practice to circulate full texts of speeches and presentations to attendees before some meetings, particularly international ones, but I'm not convinced this is really necessary. If you send them the words before a meeting, why bother delivering the speech at all? Presumably they can read. There are some benefits if people need time to ponder on, or translate, points but the practice does not contribute to sparkling sessions or much spontaneity.

Hecklers

You will, of course, need your wits about you if you get
heckled. Banner-waving protesters at mass marches and
televised meetings have unfortunately tended to encourage similar stridency at less significant public occasions.
Over-indulgence in alcohol may also lead to rather robust
behaviour by audiences so, as a public speaker, you may
have to cope with hecklers. Don't be alarmed; only a very
small minority of speakers encounter any problems.
Nevertheless, it is worth being prepared.

To counter a rowdy audience, you can simply refuse to
rise to your feet until the master of ceremonies, or
whoever else is in charge, has quelled the noise. It is not
your fault if people are noisy, so why should you bear the
brunt of the problem? At most functions it will be enough
for the chairman to say something like 'May we please
have respect for our guest?' Laying the emphasis on *guest*
may prick a few consciences.

On rising to your feet, you may be saddled with a
heckler in your audience who has either had too much to
drink or is saddled with an over-estimation of his own wit.
He may have been active during earlier speeches, which
will have given you time to consider how to handle him. If
not, ignore the first heckle unless it is a friendly and/or
amusing comment, in which case join the laughter so as
not to appear churlish. But don't respond to a more
asinine remark, other than perhaps to smile in a way
which indicates to the audience that you both know that
there is an idiot present. If there are further interruptions
you will just have to rely on your wits. If the heckler
makes a telling point on an important issue you may *have*
to respond, but don't turn it into a double act; suggest
instead that he leaves that point until the question session.
For would-be humourous interjections you could perhaps
try a rehearsed put-down; if you are expecting an
'exciting' time you could pencil a few of these (either your
own or from Part II—see pages 212-3) at the top or bottom
of your notes for quick reference. Your response *must* be
quick, but it doesn't have to be particularly funny or witty;
the fact that you have made one at all will probably get a

round of applause via which the audience can indicate its views of the heckler and, with luck, shame him into silence.

Don't lose your temper with a heckler; the audience may swing round and support him. Control him with wit and personality rather than by shouting. An imperious delivery of 'I will continue when you are quiet' will never get an audience to hush.

Your own speaking style will, to some extent, influence whether you get heckled. To adopt a blunt 'I call a spade a spade' approach will get, and may deserve, more heckling than a mellower, friendly manner.

Avoid making martyrs of hecklers. If you flatly refuse to give people a hearing at some functions, you may be playing into their hands. Their objective may simply have been to demonstrate that they were being denied a chance to speak, which may particularly apply at political meetings.

Those who have chosen to stray into this area, however, can probably handle themselves without further advice.

Questions

A speaker will often be expected to answer questions. If so and you are in doubt about whether people have heard a question, repeat it and do so without any change of emphasis. If it was a nasty one, don't try to soften it. In fact there is some merit in deliberately asking for an anticipated awkward question to be raised early in the session; the audience may be anticipating it and by raising the subject early it may help to defuse things. It may be better coming from a 'plant' than from someone who has simmered for some time before getting a chance to raise it.

Always plant a few questions in the audience, not because you expect your subject to be so dull that there won't be any, but simply to recognize that people may be reluctant to be the first to ask. A friendly, planted question will start the ball rolling. Prime one or two people by giving them a broad indication of suitable questions to ask. This will give you a chance to stress one of the areas you have covered. A planted question which has been written out in detail may sound obviously staged, however. Planted questioners should not jump in the moment you call for questions, but should pause just long enough for spontaneous ones to be asked without waiting so long that a chill settles on the room. Good timing is important.

I am not suggesting that you should totally stage-manage every function you attend but if, for example, you have an answer to a question which amuses an audience and makes a good point on which to close a session, a coded signal to a friend in the audience may be all that is required.

If you know that a member of the audience is an expert in a particular area, don't hesitate to ask him to comment, provided you know that he can be heard easily and won't go on for hours.

Despite all your planning, no questions may be forthcoming. Instead of: 'Would you like to know more about X?' (some wag may shout 'no'), try: 'Well, as we have some time left, I'd like to tell you a little more about X.' All you need do in advance is list at the end of your notes one or two other points you could make if there is time. For example, 'other countries' would remind you to talk about aspects of your subject matter in other parts of the world.

A few other points on handling questions:

- As mentioned earlier when discussing press conferences (see page 55), don't read more hostility into a question than is perhaps intended. Your questioner may be nervous and use words which sound sharper than are meant. 'What will happen to the interest on the funds deposited?' may not always imply that you plan to abscond with it.

- A question may be totally irrelevant to the subject of the meeting, in which case offer to discuss it privately afterwards or get it handled in some other way. Suppose you have spoken on motor racing to an audience in a garage showroom and someone persists in labouring on about the problem of getting a warranty claim fixed, refer him to the dealer and simply say: 'I'm sure the manager will discuss that with you during the break; now can I have another question on the subject for tonight, motor racing?'

- Don't stamp on a questioner if he asks a silly question. Let the audience come to its own conclusion that an idiot is present; don't emphasize it. Of course, before you assume a questioner is a simpleton, ask yourself if the fault lies with you for not getting the points across clearly in your speech.

Panels

As a public speaker you may occasionally appear on a panel. If so, the following notes may be useful:

- Jot down questioners' names where given so that when it comes to your turn you can address them by name. The questioner and the audience will think you are very thoughtful. Remember to write down the question too, of course, or it will be less impressed if you can't remember what was asked.

- Where questions are submitted to you or a panel in advance, you or the chairman should group them so that related topics can be covered at the same time.

- Remember to have briefing papers with you, but don't soak each questioner in a shower of statistics which you are obviously reading.

- Polite agreement with other panel members leads to a very boring function. A different view, preferably an opposing one, will make much better entertainment.

- Don't chatter to other panellists while someone else is answering a question. It will look very rude.

The law

Appearing on panels is far less nerve-racking than making speeches, but *whatever* form your public appearance takes, *don't* become so relaxed that your comments become slanderous because, without suggesting that there are pitfalls along every path you take in public speaking, it would be irresponsible not to alert you to the laws of defamation if you make inaccurate remarks about others. You are likely to be most at risk when your guard is down during an informal question and answer session, but you should avoid straying into danger at other times too.

A clearly humorous and lighthearted remark about someone who is present is unlikely to cause problems. If you say: 'I wouldn't buy even a new car from the club treasurer, let alone a secondhand one,' and grin at him as you say it, you are unlikely to come to harm (although if speaking he is likely to rib you). If your comment gets passed on secondhand, however, you could find yourself being sued; the remark would be heard in the cold light of day away from the jovial atmosphere.

Of course an audience may relish a good old slanging match between speakers on a panel, while household names automatically become butts of jokes by amateur public speakers (as well as professional comedians). It is unlikely that Hollywood lawyers will descend on you after an incautious remark about a filmstar in your speech to a train spotters' society, but you should be cautious when referring to people who may be sensitive.

A vicious personal attack, however accurate, may offend your audience and turn it against you, as will swearing. Although blasphemy is still technically against the law, no legal action is likely to be taken against you, but why upset people unnecessarily?

You will almost certainly run into trouble if you break the Official Secrets Act when speaking, although I guess it is now safe to reminisce about the happy hours you spent behind the NAAFI with that WAAF in 1943.

A final point. If you have been on an adrenalin 'high' through speaking, especially in a smoke-filled room, and you are due to drive home, it may be worth winding down by walking a few yards in the fresh air first.

14
In the chair

If you are sufficiently involved in an organization to be making speeches, then you may sooner or later be elected chairman of this or that. This chapter is devoted to the subject of chairmanship. (Yes, I know women are often in the chair, but I just can't bring myself to use that dreadful word 'chairperson'.)

A good chairman will be a leader able to command respect and keep order: he will be fair and just, tactful, calm and even-tempered. Don't worry if you don't possess all those virtues, because neither do 99 per cent of other chairmen; in fact speakers are continually swopping horror stories about bad chairmen who have lost control of dinners and other meetings. So accept the job if you are offered it because there is no reason why you shouldn't do it well, or at least as well as anyone else. The message for organizations and associations is: don't elect a chairman on the 'your turn next' principle, but pick someone with at least a few of the required attributes.

A chairman should totally immerse himself in the rules of his organization. The secretary will, or should, have them at his fingertips, but it still behoves the chairman to understand them too. For example, how many members constitute a quorum? Does the chairman have a casting vote? At some events, such as a dinner dance, a master of ceremonies or toast-master may in reality take control, but even so the chairman should keep an eye on things and keep in touch with what is happening backstage. For example, he should be told about any disaster in the kitchen which might require alteration to the timetable in order to conceal the problem from the guests.

A chairman should always arrive early so that he sets an example to the others. If he is chairing a committee meeting at which a particularly contentious matter is to be discussed, a wise chairman will do some lobbying beforehand, and he will certainly discuss with the secretary the best approach. I'm not suggesting direct manipulation, you understand—just the normal procedures which form part of our muddled but glorious democracy.

Once a function begins a chairman must make it clear that he is in charge; not with whips and cattle prods, but by having a stout gavel to bang. And bang with confidence—a timid tap on the side of a glass with a spoon is unlikely to command much respect.

Social functions, such as dinner dances, usually start 15 minutes or thereabouts after the start time on the ticket; the chairman should obviously liaise with the catering manager over this. Functions such as committee meetings should start *on time* to show people that there is business to be done. This may seem a bit heavy-handed when a small social group with only three officials are meeting in someone's kitchen, but even so it is not a bad idea to discipline yourself. If you start a meeting on time and people turn up late do make them welcome, of course, and if a large group arrives late give a quick résumé of what has happened so far.

Having banged the gavel on time, the next thing is to set the scene. After a word or two of welcome, a chairman should ensure that members know what they are there for—to resolve something or launch a fund-raising appeal, perhaps—and then his task is to keep to the agenda.

During the meeting remember the quality of fairness which is needed in a chairman. It is his job to keep the meeting on course by, for example, insisting that the committee decides *whether* to organize a particular function before discussing *when*. A chairman should not push things so fast that he rides roughshod over those who are trying to get a word in—people will only respect a dictator when he is a benevolent one. Keep your temper at all times. Cut out too much waffle. Don't let things be constantly put off to the next meeting and, at intervals, sum up 'so far' to keep the meeting on the right tack.

It is likely that a chairman will get embroiled in looking after any speakers for his organization. If so, keep the following in mind:

- Consider the balance of a list of speakers. Don't have three or four of the same type and style—vary them.

- Don't have an inordinately long list of speakers. My record is to rise to speak at 23:57; it was the only time the date has changed on my watch while speaking. As an organizer you should not over-estimate people's thresholds of boredom.

- Use word of mouth as the best way of finding speakers, but keep the circumstances in mind. If someone strongly recommends a speaker without mentioning that he heard him in action at a ribald rugby club dinner, the effect on a more genteel audience (and every audience is more genteel than a rugby one) may not be quite what you wanted.

- Put your speakers in the best order. If you have a noted humorist, place him at the end. Even if he isn't the most important speaker at least he will send your audience away happy.

- Don't forget members of your own association or club when looking for speakers; at least they will come cheap.

- Call a speaker you are considering inviting because the way he handles himself on the phone may give you a guide as to whether he is right for you.

- Be wary of well-worn speakers. I've seen some very well-known names grope in their pockets for a speech during a chairman's introduction; clearly they had made no attempt to tailor things to their audience. It's sad to see the sense of letdown in audiences on such occasions.

- If you are a bright-eyed and keen organizer, you

may be tempted to invite people to speak over a year ahead. This is totally unnecessary for most speakers and off-putting for those who have volatile schedules—they will almost certainly turn you down.

- Put your invitation to a speaker, as well as details of the occasion, in writing.

- If a speaker goes well, don't—in your euphoria— immediately invite him to come again in a year's time. Leave a day or two at least to check that everyone else shared your view of his talents and, if possible, leave a gap of a year before inviting him back.

Having sorted out speakers, you need to decide where to sit them when drawing up a seating plan (a highly sensitive area in many associations and one which will certainly involve the chairman). It makes sense to place speakers so that the microphone can be passed along the table in one direction, not backwards and forwards as various toasts are made. Ensure that serving staff do not disrupt speeches. Most caterers will want to clear the tables before speeches start anyway to avoid payment of overtime to staff who may be kept waiting.

At fairly formal functions the chairman will probably liaise with a toast-master. In theory a toast-master should ask a chairman's permission before calling on speakers to perform and the best of them will do so. But beware of those toast-masters who are too chatty and like giving speeches themselves. Work closely with your toast-master and go through exactly what he has to say.

As chairman, you will probably introduce the speakers. Give the audience enough information so that it knows who is addressing it and why, but *don't* ramble into excessive detail or effusive over-praise. Pronounce names properly and if you use first names for one speaker (which I strongly recommend, no matter how formal or pompous the occasion) use them for all; the same applies to academic or professional qualifications.

If a speaker performs poorly and starts to get a rough ride from the audience, the chairman must step in, bang his gavel and ask for respect for the speaker. If things get really rough, the chairman may have to threaten to have people ejected. The organizers of a function are, temporarily at least, the 'occupiers' of the premises where it is held and can therefore decide who may attend. Even if people turn up in response to advertisements and are therefore legally present, an organizer can still ask them to leave if their behaviour justifies it. 'Threatening, abusive or insulting words' may amount to behaviour likely to cause a breach of the peace, which is an offence. It is an offence if people are creating a disturbance to prevent the completion of business at a lawful public meeting. If they don't leave when asked they are trespassers and you are allowed to use 'reasonable force' to eject them. As this may lead to the creation of martyrs, try the softly, softly approach first. And do remember that 'reasonable force' means a firm frog-march—it does not mean you or your stewards can work the offender over in the car park later.

Where trouble is forecast, an organization should have a tactful but strong chairman and firm but understanding stewards who should protect guest speakers from verbal or physical abuse. (If the attitude of speakers starts the trouble, then it may of course be felt that they deserve all they get.)

One of a chairman's other problems may be a speaker who drones on and on, far beyond the planned time. Don't tug at his sleeve, the audience will notice. Try handing him a slip saying 'Please end in five minutes' or words to that effect. A speaker in full cry, totally fascinated with the sound of his own voice, may take offence at this but you are unlikely to invite him again anyway so no great harm will be done. Alternatively, tell a white lie and say that you had to ask him to end because the bar was closing.

If all goes well and a speaker draws to a sensible end, the chairman should lead the applause. This is particularly important if a speaker has proposed a toast because the audience may forget to applaud as it sits down again afterwards.

When a speech is followed by questions, the chairman should ask for them to be put 'through the chair' if it seems likely that things may need to be kept under firm control; obviously someone taking questions from a friendly audience may not need this protective intermediary. The chairman should not allow one questioner to hog the limelight or grind a pet axe.

Earlier it was stressed that a microphone should be used if there is any doubt about accoustics; the same applies to questioners, but there are greater problems. People, not least the person answering questioners, must be able to hear the questions, otherwise the speaker's answers may be meaningless or, worse, misleading. Floor mikes are sometimes used but these slow things down unless people queue at them to avoid long pauses between questions. Other organizations have microphones on long leads which can be passed among an audience, but these are equally unsatisfactory for the same reasons. 'Gun' mikes (highly appropriate for some questioners) which a technician can point at a questioner from some distance away are perhaps the best, but may be too high-tech and expensive for many organizations.

Where none of the above solutions appeals, either ask questioners to stand up and speak up, or have someone near the back primed to repeat questions in a loud voice. As an extra precaution a chairman should repeat (or condense) questions before these are answered. (A chairman must not attempt to shade their meaning, no matter how unfavourable to his own view the thrust may be.)

You can reduce cross-examination by asking questioners to stand up and shout—questioners can be as nervous as speakers. Incidentally, it may sometimes be appropriate for questioners to be asked to state their names and the organizations they represent.

A few other points for the chairman:

- Ask an understanding friend to have a speech in mind in case someone fails to turn up (say, to propose a toast to the guests at an annual dinner).

- A chairman should set the style in dress. He should invite gentlemen to take off their jackets if it is sweltering but should stop short of undoing a collar button and pulling down his tie—it looks scruffy.

- Try to get the feel of how a function is going and, if necessary, amend the arrangements as they progress: for example, delay a tombola if speeches are running late.

- Decide whether to have what is euphemistically called a 'comfort break' during a function, for instance after a meal but before the speeches. Guests will welcome such breaks, particularly as they get older. Better to ask guests to be back by a specific time than announce, say, a 15-minute break.

- Consider a simple signalling system to helpers which might indicate that the chairman is going to wrap things up after one more question.

- Draw up rough contingency plans in case something goes wrong. Don't lay detailed plans—the worst rarely happens—but do think in advance what to do if a speaker doesn't turn up. I suppose chairmen should also know about evacuation procedures in case of fire, but I suspect few of them do.

- There will be occasions, such as during prizegivings, when it will be helpful to have 'wallpaper' music playing to fill the silences as people walk up to collect their rewards; a helper should be on the volume control to turn the music down, or off altogether, when it is necessary for someone to speak.

- If you are involved with foreign audiences, remember that interpreters cost money so keep this in mind in your planning. For twin-town functions the struggles to grope with each other's languages will add to the warmth and fun with perhaps no formal interpreter needed. I've seen an audience greatly amused by a girl translating a torrent of Finnish into 'He says yes.' Business organizers, however, should get the best interpreters they can afford, preferably people with some knowledge of the subject/s under discussion. Position interpreters where they can see a screen if visuals are being used and don't expect them to operate efficiently for longer than half an hour or so—arrange change-overs at convenient points.

Finally, if you have chaired a function to a successful conclusion, don't just relax and forget all about it afterwards. Remember to write to key people to thank them (only around five per cent of organizations bother to write to thank speakers, by the way) and arrange a simple inquest so that your club or organization learns by its mistakes for the next time.

15
Being interviewed

Although perhaps not strictly 'public speaking', being interviewed on radio or television is an excellent way of getting across a message. But there are pitfalls, and you must understand what you are doing because the very manner in which you project your message will be as important as the message itself. People may not remember the details of what you say but they will almost certainly take away a general impression of whether you sounded honest and in touch, or evasive and shifty.

If it is all so important, should you have formal training in interview techniques? Well, professional training won't turn you into a star unless you happen to have natural talent, but it will iron out, or at least highlight, any faults. Training could therefore be useful for a businessman, if somewhat unnecessary for someone purely involved with a social group. There are several training establishments specializing in interview techniques, but they do need a commonsense approach because some seem to correct certain faults but introduce others. A common piece of advice seems to be 'get your message over come what may', but this sometimes leads the nervous into responding to a well-meaning 'good evening' with a torrent of facts and figures, which simply sounds silly. Of course you should endeavour to get your point across during an interview, but do use common sense—if an interviewer keeps asking you about job losses and you persist in side-tracking to talk about a new computer system, then don't think you will be fooling anyone. Politicians don't expect to kid people when they cynically keep side-tracking; it's one reason why they are so mistrusted.

A little DIY training using a home video as covered earlier in the book (see page 77) may be perfectly adequate for your appearance on radio or television. To go a stage further and improve your technique, ask a local radio or television reporter—the more abrasive the better—to interview you and others with a similar need, in front of a video camera if possible. This DIY approach may not be as good as a professional course but it will be a lot cheaper and will illustrate the importance of preparation and being alert.

If you know that you are to be interviewed, give some thought to the occasion and don't dash into a studio at the last minute after a hectic meeting. Be early because you won't be at your best if you have been rushing to find somewhere to park. Allow yourself plenty of time to pause and take stock.

Study the programme you have been invited to grace, establish if there will be a live audience and, where possible, listen to a previous edition to get a feel for the approach and in particular how searching the questions are likely to be. Consider *why* you have been invited to appear. Is it likely to be a kind approach because you have just announced good news, or will it be a tougher tack because you are in trouble of some sort? The programme's style will affect the amount of preparation you will need to do. You should do much more if you are likely to have a hard time and should ask friends or colleagues to throw possible awkward questions at you so that you can try out your defences. If there is an area which you are simply not prepared to talk about (perhaps because doing so would jeopardize wage negotiations or a big sale) then make this clear *before* the interview—you will look evasive if you refuse to talk about it once you are on the air. Better not to appear at all than have this happen.

Find out who else may be on the programme with you. It is better to be forewarned if a difficult and dissatisfied customer or club member is to appear or, increasingly likely, someone representing a consumer body. If a controversial issue is to be discussed there may be advantages in appearing live so that there is no risk of being poorly edited.

For a radio interview your clothing won't be seen so dress comfortably, with nothing tight around the neck. If you are appearing on television then remember that what you wear will condition what impression people have of you. If you dress in flash clothes, with jangling jewellery, people won't believe you when you say that it is not really your fault that an old couple are being evicted from your thatched cottage. You may decide to dress casually but this shouldn't mean scruffily; you won't help your message about organic foods if you have an organic growth under your fingernails and a five o'clock shadow.

Refuse any alcohol if offered before a programme because even one drink may make you slur your words. Before an interview starts you should stop smoking and cancel any bleepers on either your watch or paging system; assemble any background papers you need (for a radio interview at least) and expect to be given a voice check, with the interviewer probably asking what you had for breakfast or whether you came by bus.

During an interview:

- Concentrate.

- Listen to the questions.

- Don't pose. Be yourself.

- On television, speak to the interviewer and not to the camera.

- Remember you are there because people are interested in what you have to say so avoid clipped 'yes' and 'no' answers. Whenever possible with a recorded interview make your answers complete sentences. If asked 'How many new workers are you hiring?' don't say '24' but instead 'We will be hiring 24 new workers' because this will make editing easier. But don't ramble and don't strive too hard to be funny.

- If there is a silence remember that you don't *have* to be the first to fill it; you may jump in nervously and be indiscreet.

- Steer clear of a cosy first-name approach with the interviewer unless he is the first to start. The chummy 'Yes, Jimmy', 'No, Robin' approach of politicians being interviewed on TV can grate. If you call an interviewer 'Fred' and he replies 'Well now, Mr Smith,' the snub will be very obvious to listeners.

- If an interviewer makes an incorrect statement when asking a question or in his introduction, courteously correct it as soon as you have the chance.

- If you have an important point to make and feel you are putting it over well and the interviewer tries to chip in, keep going. Broadcasters won't like two people speaking at once and the interviewer is likely to shut up first. Again, be courteous but don't be overawed by an interviewer with an exaggerated sense of his own importance.

There's a lot to remember, but don't be put off. On most occasions things will go smoothly and you will not be subjected to any sort of third degree.

Nerves? Yes, you are likely to be a little nervous when being interviewed. The best confidence-builder is to have a firm grasp of your subject. Remember that people will not remember detail but overall impressions. The most you can hope for is to leave them thinking, 'He seems an honest bloke and knows what he's talking about so he must have a point.'

I said earlier that you should be yourself. You're not perfect, so don't be afraid to admit a mistake. Do it effectively and it will help, not hinder your cause. If you've failed to deliver a promise through bad forecasting say: 'We got it wrong, the product was even more successful than we expected. But we've taken on more people and . . .'

Now for a few more things to be aware of:

- Although an interviewer may give you an outline of his approach before a programme starts, don't expect to be given all his questions. If all goes well, try not to be thrown off stride if he then throws a final awkward question at you.

- An interviewer is unlikely to know as much about your subject as you do, so if he asks a naïve or silly question, answer him politely but briefly.

- Avoid superlatives, particularly when talking about your own product or service, and too much plugging. You will annoy the audience and won't be asked to appear again.

- Don't be too dogmatic and, while bluntness may be all very well, keep your temper if an interviewer is equally blunt, otherwise it will look as if you can dish it out but can't take it.

- Beware of slang, jargon, obscure words and percentages. In other words, avoid things which are not readily understood by the general listener or viewer.

- Get names right. It is discourteous to address someone incorrectly. You may care to jot down the names of the interviewer and any fellow guests.

- Don't bang on a table or chair arm while on air because the sound will boom out. And sit still because if you weave or bob about like a boxer, people will not be able to concentrate on your words.

- If you are appearing on a phone-in programme, brief a friend or colleague to ring in with a question if the pace slows or if the genuine questions are rather hot and you need breathing space.

- Record the interview so that you can study it afterwards and learn from your mistakes.

Be as natural as possible under the artificial conditions of a radio or television interview. Be sincere, be honest and remember that television in particular highlights deceit or evasion.

One last piece of advice: know when to stop talking.

16
Inquests

Immediately you sit down at the end of an address, the chairman or organizer is likely to say: 'Wonderful speech, old boy.' Well, he may just be being polite because he invited you in the first place, so you need to get other opinions. The length of the applause, if any, will obviously be one guide to the success of a speech, as will the financial response if you have made an appeal for funds.

A friend in the audience may be willing to eavesdrop on the comments after your speech when people are saying what they really think. If someone agrees to act as a sounding board for you ask him to look out at the same time for any unfortunate gestures or mannerisms you may have developed which distract an audience. As after-dinner speaking gets closer to up-market music hall, there is almost a case for critical reviews, exactly as for other forms of show business.

Usually the main thing to consider is whether your message got across or if further action is needed, for example, a follow-up letter to the people attending, pointing out, say, the perils of a bypass scheme and what action they should take.

A tape-recording taken during your speech will help you to judge the reaction to it. In fact, some organizers record speeches and then sell cassettes to club members. They should never do this without prior permission from speakers because to some extent the process is stealing the material from professionals who do it for a living.

Make a note of how long your speech took for future

guidance; eventually you will be able to judge that X of your bullet points equal Y minutes of speech.

Fairly soon after you have finished speaking, edit your notes so that they accurately reflect the points you made. If you left out a particular comment or joke you may be able to use it if you are invited to speak to the same audience again.

Whatever the occasion, if a speech goes all wrong, console yourself with the fact that the audience won't remember a think you said the next day anyway. I once sat through a speech by a well-known politician who got a standing ovation at the end of a brilliant conference performance. As an experiment, during coffee exactly 30 minutes after the speech I asked six people if they could remember any two of the points that had been made. None of them could. Unhappily, of course, this lack of attention also means that not too many of your messages may be remembered either, so don't fill your speech with an over-abundance of them. Never kid yourself that you are going to move mountains or bypasses with one passionate speech.

Incidentally, when you get home, remember to write a note of thanks if you have been put up for the night by one of the organizers.

Business presentations

Business presentations need even more detailed analysis afterwards. The practice is growing of sending all delegates (or a random sample of them) a questionnaire to seek their views after a meeting, and you may find this is a useful way of learning the error of your particular ways. Such a survey doesn't need to be elaborate—if it is, few people are likely to complete it—but should just have a few questions with plenty of space for delegates to add their general comments; many may be flattered to be asked for their views.

Did your message really get across? Is any further action needed? For example, if during a meeting a customer said, 'I'd like to think it over,' try to establish what particular areas are causing concern and then follow them up over the next few days.

Remember to send relevant material, plus a 'sorry you couldn't be with us' note, to absentees and, above all, follow up all promises made during the meeting.

When you've gathered all the feedback, reflect on what else will complete the presentation process. Do you need a sales incentive to improve the performances of a flagging line? Is it time to revise your discount structure? Did the meeting raise any personnel problems which need addressing? If you lost a key customer, how are you planning to win him back?

All fairly obvious points, but unless you consciously conduct a de-briefing session after a business presentation, some of them may be neglected.

Being paid to speak

Don't let your inquest turn you into a bundle of nerves about speaking again; just analyse things enough to make you better next time. You never know, you may become so good that people will be prepared to pay you to speak. Don't laugh at the idea. The demand for reasonable speakers seems inexhaustible and if you become competent then, yes, you may end up in that happy position. Consider; if you are entertaining a group of people, either by amusing or informing them, and you have had to travel or put yourself out to do so, then why shouldn't you be recompensed?

Obviously, if you are trying to sell an idea or lobby for action there will be no question of any fee, but there will be many other occasions when you can reasonably expect to get something—at the very least your expenses.

The first indication that you are about to break into the ranks of paid speakers may be a letter from an organizer with some delightfully vague phrase such as: 'Please let me know what arrangements you would like.' This probably means that they are expecting to pay, but remember: if you don't ask, you may not get.

If you are too modest to barter over your services, however, consider using an agent. The best way to find one is by asking organizers how they find their speakers; toast-masters may be another source of informtion. (Some even handle bookings themselves.) The market for speakers isn't a particularly well-organized one; for example, many large companies still rely on word of mouth to find speakers, not that this is necessarily a bad thing. It is perhaps better to rely on the opinion of someone who has heard a speaker than on an agent's hype about him.

An agent will act as a third party, which may make negotiations that much easier because he can say things in praise of your abilities which modesty would prevent you from doing. But, of course, he will want a percentage, which is likely to be negotible depending on whether you provide the lead for a booking or he does. Some agencies will charge a minimum fee to handle a booking, which is not unreasonable because dealing with over-anxious organizers can be very time-consuming.

An efficient agent will probably obtain most of the details a speaker needs but, even so, you should get the name and telephone number of a direct contact in the organization whom you can call for background information when preparing your speech.

What to charge? I can't tell you. It will depend on your ability and subject matter and, frankly, according to your star quality. Some television names are able to command very high fees.

Remember that the Inland Revenue will be interested in what you are up to. If you are in full-time employment don't rush out and spend your first fee without considering that tax will have to be paid on it (many months later). If you are self-employed, you will be able to charge such things as travelling, typing, books and papers for research and so on as expenses against the fee you earn, maybe even the use of part of your home as an office; keep these all in mind when you do your tax return. A bright accountant will be a help at this hour.

It has been known (so I'm told) for fees to be offered in cash, perhaps out of raffle proceeds. Your approach to this and the tax man has to be between you and your conscience.

I should warn you that being paid does tend to change slightly the relationship you will have with a few organizers—some make quite a ceremony of the 'handing over of the envelope' with your cheque in it. If you are using an agent, it will usually come by post later.

If you find the idea of being paid too mercenary and sordid, why not ask for a donation to your pet charity? That will solve any embarrassment and salve any problems of conscience.

17
Humour

Humour is covered in the last chapter in this section only because it is an appropriate lead-in to Part II, *not* because it is in any way unimportant; in fact, a speech can be made, or more likely, ruined, more by the use of humour than by anything else. When you laugh you take in oxygen which helps to keep you awake; it may improve circulation and even prolong your life because it helps to relieve stress. Laughter really is the best medicine and it has no side effects. This all sounds like a Good Thing for an audience, while for a speaker relaxing an audience with wit or humour may not only ensure a friendly response but may help later if you need to make a heavy point.

The approach to humour is the same whatever the occasion and the most vital thing to keep in mind is that it needs *great care*. You are far more at risk when trying to be funny than when making a serious speech. If you quote a particular statistic or make a telling point on a planning matter, then you are not necessarily seeking a positive reaction (although you may get the occasional 'hear, hear' or a few nods). But if you tell a joke you are looking for a specific response from the audience by way of smiles and, if you are lucky, laughter. If you get neither then you have failed which may embarrass you or your audience (or both) and thus dampen the occasion.

Before you decide what, if any, humour to inject into a speech, do (yet again) consider your audience because different people laugh at different things. The age, social class and, of course, nationality of your audience will affect its reaction to humour. Tired sexist jokes may not be well received by the young although anti-authority jokes could be.

Remember there is no written or unwritten rule which says that you *have* to use humour in a speech. Yes, being witty or occasionally lighthearted will stop you sounding too solemn, but a string of stories is *not* a speech. Use anecdotes or personal illustrations to lighten your address instead and if in doubt, use wit rather than humour. The difference? Well, humour is more comic, broader if you like, and less intellectual. Wit relies more on combining or contrasting previously unconnected ideas. Aristotle described it as 'cultured insolence'. A joke usually comes into the category of humour; a deadpan one-liner or a quotation from Coward or Wilde will usually be witty. (Always acknowledge your source when quoting well-known people; you don't really need to bother with unknowns.) Wit demands more of a smile than a belly laugh as a response and is therefore a lot safer than telling jokes.

Tempting though it may be to try to be humorous, fight the feeling if you know in your heart that you do not have the timing or delivery. Try things out on friends and relatives and ask them to be brutally honest. However, if you *are* a humourist but have been invited to speak on a serious topic, don't let humour swamp your message. You want them to remember your points about a bypass rather than your jokes.

If you decide to use humour despite my awful warnings, then browse through Part II of this book. But take care: it is very difficult to tell from the printed word whether the material would work for you. Would you feel comfortable telling it? Is it even suitable for you? The president of a women's organization would sound foolish telling a story which is clearly more suitable for a womanizing young bachelor and vice versa. As a challenge, write down a few random numbers, look the items up in Part II and then consider how you could conceivably link them together or build them into a speech.

Don't attempt to wade through Part II at one sitting; you will get indigestion. Take a few pages at a time and consider if something can be adapted for your purpose. And adaptation is important, so important that I have not attempted to list the material by categories; I know a lot of reference books do this but I've never used the headings and I've never met anyone else who has. At the end of the book there is an index of the items listed under subjects and under suggested occasions where they can be used but I really would recommend again that you simply dip in until you find things with which you feel comfortable.

Don't just use Part II as a source—comprehensive though I've tried to make it—but also collect clippings from newspapers and magazines of things which amuse you. The show business journals often feature advertisements from script writers who offer batches of jokes on various topics for fairly small sums, but you may find this material tired and too strong for the groups you have been asked to address.

Why not try writing something funny yourself? Impossible? Of course not. Among the funniest occasions for social groups are a mock version of a TV programme based on a group's own members, or some new, more relevant words to a popular song. The humour doesn't have to be one of the finest quality, the simple fact that it is different will entertain people (with the caveat that parodies always tend to go on just a shade too long; resist this).

You can still develop your own material for more general audiences. At the time when Nottingham police were prosecuting kerb crawlers, I said at a dinner when responding for the guests: 'I got lost coming here and stopped to ask a girl the way . . . my case comes up next week. (Pause.) Well, I didn't know I was in Hyson Green' (the area affected by the police action). If that doesn't sound funny in print it illustrates the problem in trying to judge what is funny from Part II because, believe me, it got a big laugh and a round of applause because it was topical.

Still, if you don't feel able to add your own humour to a speech and have to fall back on jokes which have done the rounds, don't despair too much. To each new generation old jokes must be new ones and anyway people seem to have short memories. In fact I have seen a comedian speak two years running to the same organization where 90 per cent of the audience was the same both years and certainly 90 per cent of his material was the same, yet he went down better the second time. Maybe people even feel affection for well-known jokes (consider how you laugh at familiar material in television repeats) although on this occasion I suspect it was a combination of food, wine and sheer chemistry, but it does illustrate what a difficult area you have strayed into when trying to entertain with humour.

Television shows use warm-up men to get an audience in the right mood before recording starts and something lighthearted fairly early on in a speech is desirable too to show that you are not such a dry old stick after all. At one function where the chairman had welcomed or introduced virtually everyone in the room, a friend of mine had the audience with him from the start by saying 'For those of you not mentioned by name, hello from me.' Be cautious in starting with a hilarious five minutes, however, and then switching abruptly into a serious quarter of an hour. Your audience may get confused because you will have struck a jarring note.

Turn a joke into a personal anecdote if you can. Instead of 'There was this man who fell off his bike,' try 'I remember when I once fell off my bike.' Then lead into the joke as if it had happened to you, *provided* it is apposite. The worst words in any speech are: 'That reminds me of the story about . . .' or 'There was this salesman . . .' because you have signalled that you are launching into a joke and such stories are never relevant anyway. The more you can work material *into* your speech the better it will work.

Beware of long, complicated jokes. You are more likely to get them wrong; people's agony will be prolonged if they have heard them before or you tell them badly, and if you 'die' in telling a long joke you will die in a big way and your speech may perish too. You are much less at risk with a crisp one-line comment. If you want something longer then a joke which builds up is better than one which is hopelessly involved. An old example of a build-up joke is to say, 'I am sorry that (pick someone who is currently famous but not for his or her intellect) can't be with us tonight. He had a fire at his home last week and his library burnt down. Both books were destroyed.' Pause—some, if not all, of the audience will laugh—then say, 'Which was a pity because he'd only coloured in one of them.'

And that further highlights two of the points I've made: it isn't funny in print and it is very old, but it is invariably well received. Obviously with an example like that you would have to choose the right person to rib. And don't mock the cherished traditions of the group you are addressing (especially regiments), unless you are able to do so very affectionately.

As well as build-up jokes, 'sting in the tail' comments may also be well received. For instance: 'Where would we be without our wives? (Pause.) Gleneagles?' Or: 'The legal profession is part of our great tradition, like the stocks and the Bloody Tower . . . and some solicitors should be put in both.' Or perhaps write a very twee poem, with a sting in an unexpected last line. Or make the last line equally twee and then attribute it to a totally inappropriate figure, such as a trade union leader currently in bad odour.

Avoid sarcasm, it is rarely funny, but do use topicality. It will show you are in touch with life and your audience will think what clever people they are for spotting the reference too. There are two provisos:

- Don't refer to news which broke at 7 p.m. if you are speaking at 7.30, because few in the room may have heard it.

- Avoid topical subjects which are only known to a few of those present, for instance at a professional meeting at which the majority are guests. The reference may irritate those not in the know because their lack of understanding will make them feel just slightly ignorant, whereas your aim should be to keep people relaxed and entertained.

Perhaps the most important word on the subject of humour is 'timing'. The ability to time a joke or comment really well is perhaps inborn, as is the ability to be a good organizer; if someone doesn't sense intuitively that a room needs a microphone, then it shows a lack of basic feel for the subject. But it is possible to improve your timing with experience and you will come to sense, if you get a laugh, whether you should cut in and carry on (thus bringing some laughter to a premature end) or wait until it all dies down, which may mean that those who stopped laughing first have been waiting with their attention flagging.

Recognize that a joke will fail occasionally, however well told, because another speaker may have told it or it has been well used in the area; it may be worth telling your neighbours over dinner what jokes you plan to use to see if they have heard them or know if they have been well aired locally. The mood of an audience can affect the response to humour, as can the seating. If you are too far away it will be more difficult to strike a rapport; some venues are notoriously bad. Anyway if a piece of humour fails, don't immediately plough straight into another but get the audience's confidence back with some general chat first.

Be grateful for any unexpected laugh—you may stumble into something unknown to you but known to the audience. But if a speech is going well *don't* add new material or go on too long. The finest sound you can hear as a speaker is 'more'.

It is easy to get carried away and mistake joke-telling for public speaking (although there are occasions, like the much-maligned rugby club, where the two may be synonymous) so to keep your feet on the ground, here are some 'don'ts'.

- Don't read jokes, even if you are reading the rest of your speech. They will sound forced and will lack spontaneity.

- Don't put your punch line first. If you do, why bother telling the joke?

- Don't giggle or laugh at your own comments.

- Don't signal that something is supposed to be funny. 'Here's a good one' is guaranteed to turn people off.

- Tailor jokes to your audience, but remember that professional groups will almost certainly have heard all the jokes about their specialist world.

- Don't pun. Very occasionally a pun will amuse; more often your audience will groan and its distress will be fairly genuine.

- Don't do impersonations unless you are very sure of yourself (perhaps not even then). And be wary of attempting accents too.

- Don't fall in love with a joke. If you think something is very funny but it never gets a reaction from an audience, drop it.

- Don't forget that if you rib other people you must be able to take a joke against yourself.

Remember that the order in which you narrate something may affect how humorous it is. As an example, a friend with four daughters planned to start a speech by saying: 'I'm delighted to be here because it is unusual for me to be able to get a word in edgeways as I've got four daughters.' He reversed the order to: 'I've got four daughters so it is a delight for me to come somewhere where I can get a word in edgeways' and it worked much better. Now, before women's groups start shouting 'male chauvinist pig', let me point out that while no-one is claiming that it was one of the great *bon mots* of our time, it was well-received by a mixed audience and made a pleasant introduction. So always consider if you can improve something by re-arranging it.

Finally, consider the boundaries of taste when using humour. Four-letter words are regularly used on television, but I would not consider using them in this book and I don't think you should use them when making speeches. A comic or an actor playing a part may get away with them (although all too often they are used to conceal the paucity of humour in whatever they embellish) but you may not, not least because you will be uneasy using them.

Risqué stories are a different matter and one or two (not a string) will be enjoyed by most audiences, however starchy the organizer may have made them sound in his invitation to you. Best of all, if you can find them, are stories which appear as if they are going to be rather broad but turn out to be totally clean. If there is sexual content to a story it is better implied than boldly set out; if in doubt, don't go too far. Except for classic 'stag' functions where they are the norm, it is probably best not to use blue jokes.

It is puzzling that hen parties are growing in popularity because it seems to me that, as women make their way in so many professions, previously exclusively male, the stag function must eventually die. Perhaps I'm wrong and it just illustrates that good honest vulgarity—on which after all, much of the world's humour is based—is healthily therapeutic. But do recognize that attitudes change so avoid 'mother-in-law' jokes (you won't find any in Part II) or any sexist material for that matter. Yes, comedians still use it and, yes, it still works, but it probably won't for you. Nor will 'jokes' about people with speech impediments.

There are a few other points on taste to remember:

- Avoid lavatorial humour.

- Don't joke about the handicapped (although *they* can be very funny on the subject).

- Avoid religious jokes, unless they gently illustrate a point or if you can honestly say, for instance, about a Jewish story that 'This was told to me by a rabbi.'

- Be cautious with ethnic humour. I know professional comedians use it very successfully, but an amateur speaker telling too many Irish jokes can be very wearisome. (The Irish ought to object on grounds of boredom not just defamation of character.) That said, virtually every nation tells jokes about a neighbouring country, portraying the people as dim—the Swiss joke about Austrians, the French about the Belgians; and it even happens *within* countries, for example in the west of Austria they joke about people from Burgenland in the east, while in Italy, Romans joke about the Milanese and vice versa.

- Humour should not be taken too seriously but the growth of racist material is less than savoury. Don't join in.

Be doubly cautious with foreign audiences; as Mark Twain said, 'A German joke is no laughing matter.' Use wit rather than broad humour and try to get a national to check that you are not going to blunder into *double entendre*. British people speaking to foreign audiences perhaps start with an advantage in that, almost without exception, foreigners admire what they call 'the English sense of humour'—it tends to be seen as self-mocking, civilized and to some extent sophisticated. Even so, be cautious in using humour. Discuss it with locals first and keep in mind that you will be on safer ground in ribbing your own rather than other countries.

Finally, whether speaking to a foreign or domestic audience, remember you don't *have* to tell jokes when making a speech.

PART II

Using the material

Please read the following notes *before* using the material in Part II:

- If you haven't read Part I of the book then consider doing so because it will guide you on how to structure a speech and build in humour. A string of jokes with no real link does *not* make a speech!

- Do keep your audience in mind when attempting to use humour—some may need a more robust approach than others. Keep in mind too that the *mix* of the audience may affect what you can use; if they are mainly casual guests (rather than members of a specific group) then 'in' jokes or references will be lost on them; you will be on safer ground ribbing the venue or food, or joking about topical events in the outside world.

- The quality of what you say is more important than the quantity. Don't cram in too many jokes or quotes; just use enough to brighten your address.

- Make your references *apt* and where necessary *adapt* the material so that it suits your theme and your audience. To help you, some of the material has 'X's to indicate that you should use local names; other material has items in brackets, again to indicate that you should adapt for your use. '. . .' in the material indicates where pauses could perhaps come when you are delivering it.

- The material is *deliberately* listed in random order to encourage you to dip in and adapt. However, if you want more help then the Index lists the items under subject headings.

- Although you should avoid long convoluted anecdotes, do remember that some jokes need word pictures painting for the punch line to work; just don't paint for too long. Bear in mind that some words are funny in themselves; don't ask me why, but 'prat', for instance, is and it perfectly describes someone who is one.

- A final point: any selection of material like this must, to some extent, reflect the sense of humour of the compiler. I like sharp, pointed humour but I guess too much of it could perhaps make you sound more brittle than you really are. Choose some of the gentler quotations or other material if you feel this is a risk.

Material for speeches

1 Wit is a sword; it is meant to make people feel the point as well as see it.

G. K. Chesterton

2 Brevity is the soul of wit.

Shakespeare

3 Speech is great, but silence is greater.

Carlyle

4 Speeches cannot be made long enough for the speakers, nor short enough for the hearers.

Perry

5 If they haven't heard it before, it's original.

Gene Fowler

6 A man commented in a bar that the only thing that had ever come out of (town) were tarts and rugby players. Someone standing nearby angrily interjected that his wife came from (town).
First man: 'Really? What position does she play?'

7 The doctors told him to eat more fruit . . . so he now has two cherries in his Martinis.

8 It's easier to forgive an enemy once you've got even with him.

9 He's a well balanced (Yorkshire) man . . . he has a chip on each shoulder.

10 Every dogma has its day.

11   A woman drove me to drink and I never even had the courtesy to thank her.

W. C. Fields

12   Marriage as an institution is fine . . . for those who like living in institutions.

13   To me, old age is always 15 years older than I am.

Bernard M. Baruch

14   Sex is not taxed, but it can be taxing.

John Barrymore

15   Thank you for that spontaneous . . . apathy.

16   I always keep a supply of stimulant handy in case I see a snake—which I also keep handy.

W. C. Fields

17   It's not the men in my life that counts, it's the life in my men.

Mae West

18   He plays golf religiously . . . every Sunday.

19   Here lie the bones of Elizabeth Charlotte,
That was born a virgin and died a harlot.
She was aye a virgin till seventeen—
An extraordinary thing for Aberdeen.

20   The British have a remarkable talent for keeping calm, even when there is no crisis.

Franklin P. Jones

21   When Gandhi was asked what he thought of western civilization, he replied that he believed it would be a very good idea.

22   Conscience is the inner voice that warns us that somebody may be watching.

H. L. Mencken

23   A Kinsey report on sexual intercourse found an average frequency of 2.4 times per week. My friend's wife reckons he gets the 2, she gets the ·4.

24 Elections are held to delude the populace into believing that they are participating in government.

Gerald F. Lieberman

25 He's the only person I know who uses third-class stamps.

26 I don't know what effect these men may have on the enemy, but by Gad, they frighten me!

Duke of Wellington

27 Since a politician never believes what he says, he is always astonished when others do.

Charles de Gaulle

28 He works very hard. He really burns the midday oil.

29 George the First was always reckoned
Vile, but viler George the Second;
And what mortal ever heard
Any good of George the Third?
When from earth the Fourth descended
(God be praised!) the Georges ended.

Walter Savage Lander

30 Under a sign reading 'Free Wales', someone has written 'From what? For what?'

31 Political power grows out of the barrel of a gun.

Mao Tse-Tung

32 Praise undeserved is satire in disguise.

Broadhurst

33 If the world had piles I always feel this would be where they'd be.

34 They held a beauty contest there last week . . . and nobody won.

35 I don't like her. But don't misunderstand me: my dislike is purely platonic.

Sir Herbert Beerbohm Tree

36 The circus strongman bent iron bars, lifted weights and finally squeezed a lemon until he claimed there wasn't a drop left in it. At this a weedy little man stepped forward, squeezed the lemon and got another spoonful out of it. As the applause died down he modestly explained that he was a local tax collector (or accountant at a company you are addressing).

37   Some people have a foolish way of not minding, or pretending not to mind, what they eat. For my part, I mind my belly very studiously and very carefully; for I look upon it that he who does not mind his belly will hardly mind anything else.

Samuel Johnson

38   Men are seldom more innocently employed than when they are honestly making money.

Samuel Johnson

39   The train was so crowded that even some of the men couldn't get seats.

40   A German general asked an English officer why the English always won wars even though there was little difference in forces. 'Because we pray to God before each battle,' said the Englishman. 'But we do, too,' said the German. Englishman: 'Surely you don't expect God to understand German, do you?'

41   Dear Grandmamma, with what we give,
We humbly pray that you may live
For many, many happy years:
Although you bore us all to tears.

Hilaire Belloc

42   This is a very small joke . . . and one in which I am rapidly losing confidence.

43   A classic is something everybody wants to have read and no-one wants to read.

Mark Twain

44   When God created Switzerland, He and the first Swiss stood drinking glasses of milk from the first Swiss cow, surveying the wonderful scenery.
'Will there be anything else, my son?' asked God.
'Not really, just the 10 francs for your glass of milk, please.'

45 On an interminable train journey, plagued with delays, a girl rushed up to the guard and asked him to stop the train because she was going to have a baby. He chided her for boarding the train in that condition. She pointed out that she hadn't been in that condition when she started the journey.

46 Ladies and gentlemen, I give you [X]. And you can keep it.

47 He comes from such an old family he claims an ancester was a hod-carrier on Hadrian's Wall.

48 Of the delights of this world, man cares most for sexual intercourse, yet he has left it out of his heaven.

Mark Twain

49 The message arrived by a happy motorcycle courier. I knew he was happy because he'd got greenfly on his teeth.

50 Twenty years of romance make a woman look like a ruin; but twenty years of marriage make her something like a public building.

Oscar Wilde

51 (The elements of this (old!) story—airline or train, name of hotel, and so on—can be selected and embroidered to suit the audience. But don't make it over-long.)
A man commented in the hairdresser's that he was going to Italy and hoped to see the Pope. The barber criticized his proposed method of travel, the hotel he planned to use and finally said he had no chance of ever seeing the Pope.
When he got back from Rome the barber asked how he'd got on. The man explained that everything had worked out fine and that he *had* got to see the Pope.
'What did the Pope say to you?' asked the barber.
'Who on earth gave you that awful haircut?'

52 Apparently the government is to give tax relief on vasectomies . . . because it wants to encourage more cuts in the private sector.

53 The trumpets sounded.
Jesus said 'Come'

The pearly gates opened
And in walked Mum.

54 No-one is exempt from talking nonsense; the misfortune is to do it solemnly.

Montaigne

55 I thought the food was fit for the gods . . . if they don't mind getting wind.

56 A bore is a person who talks when you want him to listen.

Ambrose Bierce

57 The length of a meeting rises with the square of the number of people present.

Eileen Shanahan

58 It's such an honest town, Securicor runs mopeds.

59 His death, which happened in his berth,
At 40-odd befell:
They went and told the sexton, and
The sexton tolled the bell.

Thomas Hood

60 There was a thought that an explorer could perhaps address you instead of me today. The Explorers' Society gave us the name of someone who claimed to have been through hell in a primitive distant land. But when we investigated we found the bloke had simply been a (sales rep) in (Cornwall) when X (for example, present managing director) was district manager.

61 First man: 'How's your wife?'
Second man: 'Compared with whose?'

62 A Christian is someone who is stoical in the face of another's misfortune.

Alexander Pope

63 She said she refused to be dictated to . . . then promptly became a secretary.

64 An Irishman (or any other race you wish to portray as relaxed) was asked by a Spaniard if there was an Irish equivalent of *mañana*. The Irishman thought and said, 'Yes, several, but none of them really conveys the same sense of urgency.'

65   In the adversity of our best friends we often find something that is not exactly displeasing.

La Rochefoucauld

66   This (venue) looks like the sort of thing God would have done . . . if he'd had money.

67   In my experience, if you have to keep the lavatory door shut by extending your left leg, it's modern architecture.

Nancy Banks Smith

68   May you live all the days of your life.

Jonathan Swift

69   If the speech goes well I'll be invited back next year. If it goes *very* well I won't have to eat the meal.

70   A memorial in a church in India reads:
'Sacred to the memory of Brigadier Lancelot David Warnock of the Royal Hussars, who was accidentally killed by his batman on October 5th, 1872.
Well done, thou good and faithful servant.'

71   He looked like a composite picture of five thousand orphans too late to catch a picnic steamboat.

O. Henry

72   He's been stopped so often for speeding, the police have given him a season ticket.

73   In advertising terms, an intellectual is anybody who reads a morning newspaper.

Anna-Maria Winchester

74   Our company is dominated by the finance man. An example: I was in the cashier's office yesterday morning when robbers burst in and made everyone lie face down on the floor. A pretty clerk arrived late, saw what we were doing and lay on her back at the end of the line. I heard the cashier whisper to her, 'Turn over, Mary, it's a bank raid . . . not the auditors.'

75   The first half of our life is ruined by our parents and the second half by our children.

Clarence Darrow

76   We will soon reach the stage where we only have elections to see if the opinion polls were right.

77   I've never seen his moustache looking in such fine condition. The last time I saw a growth like that on a top lip . . . the whole herd had to be destroyed.

78   I think I have convincingly demonstrated the art of the politician—I've spoken for several minutes without actually saying anything.

79   A glassblower lies here at rest
Who one day burst his noble chest
While trying, in a fit of malice,
To blow a second Crystal Palace

J. B. Morton

80   The problem with America is that their toilet paper is too thin and their newspapers too fat.

Winston Churchill

81   Clearly you are my kind of audience . . . no taste.

82   Never despise what it says in the women's magazines; it may not be subtle but neither are men.

Zsa Zsa Gabor

83   We've introduced flexitime—you can come in any time you like before 8 and leave whenever you like after 6.30.

84   Always forgive your enemies—nothing annoys them so much.

Oscar Wilde

85   A girl went to a clairvoyant for lessons and towards the end of the visit he told her to take her clothes off. As she did so, she said, 'I think I know what's going to happen now.'

'There you are,' said the clairvoyant, 'And you've only had one lesson!'

86 A businessman, in deep trouble, decided that prayer was his only hope, but when he entered a church and knelt, he found a tramp in rags loudly praying alongside him. Resourceful to the last, the businessman thrust £10 at the tramp, shooed him out of the church, turned to the altar and said, 'Now, Lord, that I have your undivided attention . . .'

87 Middle age is when you are sitting at home on a Saturday night and the telephone rings and you hope it isn't for you.

Ogden Nash

88 (Useful for a reference to expense accounts on business occasions.)
Nobody was ever meant
To remember or invent
What he did with every cent.

Robert Frost

89 About the only people who don't get customers coming back complaining are parachute manufacturers.

90 Acting is hell: you spend all your time trying to do what they put people in asylums for.

Jane Fonda

91 I think it's always been a source of embarrassment to him that he was born in bed with a woman.

92 The trouble with our times is that the future is not what it used to be.

Paul Valéry

93 If all the world loves a lover, why do policemen go around shining torches into dark corners?

94 A speech does not have to be eternal to be immortal.

95 An idealist is a man with both feet planted firmly in the air.

Franklin D. Roosevelt.

96 (If following a brilliant speech)
X and I agreed that we would swap speeches tonight, so here is his.

97 The doctor gave me just three months to live but when I didn't pay his bill he was very understanding . . . he gave me another three months.

98 Ask not what you can do for your country, for they are liable to tell you.

Mark Steinbeck

99 Advertising may be described as the science of arresting the human intelligence long enough to get money from it.

Stephen Leacock

100 He doesn't sleep too well and his doctor has told him to count up to a thousand when he goes to bed to help him relax. Unfortunately he's an ex-boxer . . . so he jumps up out of bed every time he gets to nine.

101 Never go to bed mad. Stay up and fight.

Phyllis Diller

102 Answering the question 'Do you use your car for pleasure?' on the application form for third party fire and theft insurance, the young man put 'Only if I can't borrow my friend's flat.'

103 A fanatic is someone who can't change his mind and won't change the subject.

Winston Churchill

104 Things could be worse . . . I could be here in person.

105 A university is a place where pebbles are polished and diamonds are dimmed.

Ingersoll

106 What is the difference between a pigeon and a stockbroker (or any group in the news because of adversity)? A pigeon can still put down a deposit on a Porsche.

107 Then later we will have a Quaker waltz—twice round the floor then outside for your oats.

108 A real patriot is the fellow who gets a parking ticket and rejoices that the system works.

Bill Vaughn

109 He doesn't stop the show . . . he just slows it up.

110 I've always felt that a person's intelligence is directly reflected by the number of conflicting points of view he can entertain simultaneously on the same topic.

Lisa Alther

111 Under a sign outside a church reading 'Where will *you* be on Judgement Day?' someone has scribbled '*Still* waiting for a number 14 bus.'

112 (After the toast-master has banged loudly before introducing you)
The last time someone banged like that, my brother-in-law was sent down for six months.

113 Lord Finchley tried to mend the Electric Light
Himself. It struck him dead: And serves him right!
It is the business of the wealthy man
To give employment to the artisan.

Hilaire Belloc

114 I don't wish to be disrespectful to the law, but how can you take it really seriously when grown men don wigs and red dresses . . . and then admonish others for deviant sexual behaviour?

115 I understand that astronauts are now training in (show-room of someone you want to rib or of a keen business rival) . . . because they need a place with no atmosphere.

116 He thought the Trough of Bowland was a pig farm.

117 To love oneself is the beginning of a life-long romance.

Oscar Wilde

118 He just sat there reading *The Invisible Man*. The illustrated edition, of course.

119 It's the little questions from women about tappets that finally push men over the edge.

Philip Roth

120 Times are so hard, his car phone is on a party line.

121 'My country, right or wrong' is a thing no patriot would think of saying except in a desperate case. It is like saying, 'My mother, drunk or sober!'

G. K. Chesterton

122 At the end of an acrimonious paternity case, the judge pondered then solemnly handed the defendant a cigar and said, 'Congratulations, you have just become a father.'

123 Men have sight; women insight.

Victor Hugo

124 An archbishop is a Christian who has attained a rank superior to that of Christ.

H. L. Mencken

125 It is said that what X lacks in size, he makes up for in speed. The sad thing is that it's his wife who says it.

126 Her voice was ever soft, gentle, and low—an excellent thing in woman.

Shakespeare

127 The Delphic oracle said I was the wisest of all the Greeks. It is because that I alone, of all the Greeks, know that I know nothing.

Socrates

128 Patriotism is the last refuge of a scoundrel.

Samuel Johnson

129 His family, though long established, never actually had a family curse. In fact for many years they thought X was it.

130 When a women turns to scholarship there is usually something wrong with her sexual apparatus.

Friedrich Nietzsche

131 You have to admire the way he . . . sank to the occasion.

132 A lady of a 'certain age', which means certainly aged.

Lord Byron

133   (A tongue-in-cheek grace)
Gentle Jesus, Lord Divine
Who turneth water into wine
Please forgive these foolish men
Who seek to turn it back again.

134   What should a girl give a man who has everything?
Encouragement.

135   People who bite the hand that feeds them usually
lick the boot that kicks them.

Eric Hoffer

136   Sex education may be a good idea in the schools but I
don't believe the kids should be given homework.

Bill Cosby

137   He was so mean he finally strangled himself . . .
trying to get cider from his Adam's apple.

138   People generally quarrel because they cannot argue.

G. K. Chesterton

139   When our personnel officer was ill he received a
message from the branch secretary of the union reading,
'This is to wish you a complete and rapid recovery. P.S.
This was carried by nine votes to seven.'

140   We were planning to count the candles on his
birthday cake . . . but we were driven back by the heat.

141   I'm Smith of Stoke, aged 60-odd,
I've lived without a dame
From youth-time on: and would to God
My dad had done the same.

Thomas Hardy

142   It is inexcusable for scientists to torture animals; let
them make their experiments on journalists and politicians.

Henrik Ibsen

143   I could tell the previous speaker was a golfer by the
way he held the mike with an interlocking grip.

144   The thing we have to fear in this country, to my way of thinking, is the influence of the organized minorities, because somehow or other the great majority does not seem to organize. They seem to feel that they are going to be effective because of their own strength, but they give no expression of it.

Alfred E. Smith

145   A woman who moralizes is invariably plain.

Oscar Wilde

146   Apparently she carries all her money about in her tight-fitting jumper. She reckons it draws more interest there.

147   Women over 30 are at their best, but men over 30 are too old to recognize it.

Jean-Paul Belmondo

148   Adam was the only man who, when he said a good thing, knew that nobody had said it before him.

Mark Twain

149   The distance between twin beds: a cock stride, or a lover's leap.

150   A woman's mind is cleaner than a man's; she changes it more often.

Oliver Herford

151   I don't say he is a bad cook. I just wonder if shepherd's pie is *supposed* to glow in the dark.

152   The wrong sort of people are always in power because they would not be in power if they were not the wrong sort of people.

Jon Wynne-Tyson

153   Children certainly brighten up a home. Mainly because they never turn the lights off.

154   Anyone who knows anything of history knows that great social changes are impossible without the feminine upheaval. Social progress can be measured exactly by the social position of the fair sex; the ugly ones included.

Karl Marx

155 Wanting to express disapproval of a document, a manager was tempted to write a rude word on it. Instead he put 'Round objects'.

Several days later it came back with a memo asking 'Who is Mr Round and what does he object to?'

156 I'm afraid X can't be here today. It was a full moon last night.

157 If you want to kill any idea in the world today, get a committee working on it.

C. F. Kettering

158 A mother takes 20 years to make a man of her boy and another woman makes a fool of him in 20 minutes.

Robert Frost

159 The secretary has asked me to tell you that the mystery tour has had to be cancelled . . . the coach driver has lost his blindfold.

160 Everybody talks about the weather but nobody does anything about it.

Mark Twain

161 I am free of all prejudices. I hate everyone equally.

W. C. Fields

162 When the cat burglar shinned down the drainpipe and returned to his friend on watch at the gate, he explained that he hadn't got anything because the house belonged to a tax inspector. 'Did you *lose* anything then?' asked the guard.

163 The music teacher came twice each week to bridge the awful gap between Dorothy and Chopin.

George Ade

164 He's never been much of a sportsman. When he played in goal at football the team called him Cinderella . . . because he kept missing the ball.

165   Early to rise and early to bed makes a male healthy and wealthy and dead.

James Thurber

166   He was a premature baby . . . his father wasn't expecting him.

167   Soldiers can win battles and generals get the medals.

Napoleon Bonaparte

168   There was a fire in one of the plane's engines. But, typically, he didn't panic . . . it wasn't on his side.

169   As soon as I arrived your chairman/toast-master took me to one side . . . and left me there.

170   Later we will be hearing from the treasurer . . . and his accomplices.

171   You can't learn too soon that the most useful thing about a principle is that it can always be sacrificed to expediency.

W. Somerset Maugham

172   Those are my principles, but if you can't accept them, I have others.

173   As for the virtuous poor, one can pity them, of course, but one cannot admire them.

Oscar Wilde

174   He claims he got a Blue at Oxford. And if someone hadn't jogged his arm he thinks he would have probably got the pink and black as well.

175   The office of President is such a bastardized thing, half-royalty and half-democracy, that nobody knows whether to genuflect or spit.

Jimmy Breslin

176   After he left school he started work with a local company and after six months the chairman called him in and said, 'We have decided you are the one who should go on a Harvard business course and then come back here as managing director.' He was overwhelmed and said, 'Thanks . . . Dad.'

177   Well, it's hard for a mere man to believe that a woman doesn't have equal rights.

Dwight D. Eisenhower

178   I had just dozed off into a stupor when I heard what I thought was myself talking to myself. I didn't pay much attention to it, as I knew practically everything I would have to say to myself, and wasn't particulary interested.

Robert Benchley

179   The coffee here is blended. Monday's blended with Tuesday's.

180   A bore is a man who, when you ask him how he is, tells you.

Bert Leston Taylor

181   I won't say he's mean but when he got lost in the Alps and a Red Cross St Bernard found him, he sent it back with a note tied to its collar reading, 'I gave already.'

182   A vice-president is a person who finds a molehill on his desk in the morning and must make a mountain out of it by 5 p.m.

Fred Allen

183   A lecturer said, 'We will now consider the number of ways of making love.' A wag at the back shouted '51'. Undeterred, the lecturer continued, 'In the first position the man lies on top of the woman.' Voice: '52'.

184   The race is not always to the swift, nor the battle to the strong, but that's the way to bet.

Damon Runyon

185   His parents were so poor they had to buy his clothes from Army & Navy surplus. In fact, until he was 11 he thought he was a Japanese admiral.

186   We know what happens to people who stay in the middle of the road. They get run over.

Aneurin Bevan

187   A foreman was interviewing an Irishman for a building job and to test his general knowledge asked the difference between a girder and a joist. 'Well', said the Irishman, 'Girder wrote *Faust* and Joist wrote *Ulysses*.'

188   I don't want to own anything that won't fit into my coffin.

Fred Allen

189   Parents are the last people on earth who ought to have children.

Samuel Butler

190   He's been offered a part in a film about the Romans, as a centurion. They reckon he looks like a tank.

191   When he who hears does not know what he who speaks means, and when he who speaks does not know what he himself means—that is philosophy.

Voltaire

192   Critics are like eunuchs in a harem: they know how it's done, they've seen it done every day, but they're unable to do it themselves.

Brendan Behan

193   In a tough night club a slightly seedy singer was being given a rough ride. Amidst the cries of 'rubbish' and 'get off', a large man rose and shouted 'Be quiet—give the poor old cow a chance.' At which the singer simpered: 'Thank you. I'm glad to see there's one gentleman in the place.'

194   Democracy means simply the bludgeoning of the people by the people for the people.

Oscar Wilde

195   A very traditional American politician called the local military base and asked them to set up two officers to fill sudden gaps in a dinner party. He added 'And no Polacks'.

   At the appointed hour two tall and dignified soldiers apeared, both black. When the senator commented that their commanding officer had perhaps made a mistake, one of the officers replied 'That's not possible, sir. Commander Walchowski never makes mistakes.'

196   Music hath charm to soothe a savage beast—but I'd try a revolver first.

Josh Billings

197 One of the first and most important things for a critic to learn is how to sleep undetected at the theatre.

William Archer

198 He went to the ballet . . . and complained he couldn't hear a word.

199 A woman without a man is like a fish without a bicycle.

Gloria Steinem

200 An insistent market researcher buttonholed a man and asked him what he ate, what car he drove and so on, and finally asked how often he made love. When the man answered 'Seven times a year,' the researcher commented that that wasn't very often, to which the man replied 'Well, I don't think it's too bad for a Catholic priest in a small community.'

201 Any girl can be glamorous. All you have to do is stand still and look stupid.

Hedy Lamarr

202 Here lies my wife
Here let her lie!
Now she's at rest
And so am I.

John Dryden (proposed epitaph for his wife)

203 The flush toilet is the basis of western civilization.

Alan Coult

204 First schoolchild: 'Mummy says we've got to be quiet because Grandma is reading the Bible.'
Second schoolchild: 'Swotting for her finals?'

205 Nothing soothes me more after a long and maddening course of pianoforte recitals than to sit and have my teeth drilled.

George Bernard Shaw

206 At least that introduction was better than the last time when the toast-master asked me, 'Are you ready to speak now . . . or shall we let them enjoy themselves a bit longer?'

207   I get my exercise acting as a pall-bearer to my friends who exercise.

Chauncey Depew

208   Our football team was so bad that when we got a corner we were allowed to do a lap of honour.

209   He walks down Lovers' Lane . . . holding his own hand.

210   No-one should have to dance backward all their lives.

Jill Ruckelshaus

211   The chef here treats guests like gods . . . he keeps putting burnt offerings before them.

212   Of all the wonders of nature, a tree in summer is perhaps the most remarkable; with the possible exception of a moose singing 'Embraceable You' in spats.

Woody Allen

213   Journalism: a profession whose business it is to explain to others what it personally does not understand.

Lord Northcliffe

214   (Dismal seaside town) is so dull, the tide went out one day and didn't bother to come back.

215   The English instinctively admire any man who has no talent and is modest about it.

James Agee

216   Bernard Shaw once said that he thought youth is wasted on the young.

217   Men have a much better time of it than women. For one thing they marry later; for another they die earlier.

H. L. Mencken

218   Niagara Falls is only the second biggest disappointment of the standard honeymoon.

Oscar Wilde

219   I always travel by X airline (or on X ships) because there's none of that nonsense about women and children first.

220 He thought camiknickers were people who steal soap.

221 What did the Indians call America before the white man came? Ours.

222 For those of you who have had a heavy day, I've booked an alarm call for the end of my speech.

223 Having spent my entire vacation in a nudist colony, I was somewhat taken back when a lady shook my hand and said: 'Goodbye, Mr Nunn. I hope to see more of you.'

Gregory Nunn

224 We were hoping to have (someone with distinctive voice) here tonight . . . but he gives elocution lessons on (Mondays).

225 He's very community-minded. So much so that the council have got him earmarked for a key role if there's another war . . . as a hostage.

226 A man marries to have a home, but also because he doesn't want to be bothered with sex and all tht sort of thing.

W. Somerset Maugham

227 If he is ever in trouble I'll be the first to dial 998.

228 Adam came first—but then men always do.

229 I told the waiter there was a fly on my ice cream. He said it had come for the winter sports.

230 Women give themselves to God when the devil wants nothing more to do with them.

Sophie Arnould

231 Why is it that a slight tax increase costs you £100 yet what the Chancellor calls a substantial tax cut only saves you £1.75?

232 He's as broke as the Ten Commandments.

233 His indecision was final.

234 A man in love is incomplete until he has married. Then he's finished.

Zsa Zsa Gabor

235 He's a modest man . . . but then he has a lot to be modest about.

236 I shall marry in haste and repeat at leisure.

James Branch Cabell

237 I remember when this club was in its infancy, it ran a pet show which was so poorly supported that someone won first prize with a tin of salmon.

238 Work is the curse of the drinking class.

Oscar Wilde

239 This evening has been the most fun I've ever had . . . without laughing.

240 The House of Lords is a perfect eventide home.

Baroness Mary Stocks

241 Anything that is too stupid to be spoken is sung.

Voltaire

242 Their sex drive is so low that the only time they even get fun out of holding hands is when they are playing cards.

243 If one man says to thee, 'Thou art a donkey,' pay no heed. If two speak thus, purchase a saddle.

The Talmud

244 When a waiter died his widow went to a seance to try to make contact with him. When knocking noises came from the table the woman said, 'If that's you George, please speak to me.' An ethereal voice replied 'I'm sorry, I can't, that's not my table.'

245 He missed an invaluable opportunity to hold his tongue.

Andrew Lang

246 Why does a woman work 10 years to change a man's habits and then complain that he's not the man she married?

Barbra Streisand

247 He got badly knocked about fighting for a girl's honour. She was very anxious to keep it.

248   A person who can break wind is not dead.

Jean-Jacques Rousseau

249   When a girl marries, she exchanges the attentions of many men for the inattention of one.

Helen Rowland

250   The last time I spoke in public the audience was with me all the way. I managed to shake it off when we reached the motorway.

251   The covers of this book are too far apart.

Ambrose Bierce

252   A lecturer is someone who talks in another person's sleep.

253   Man—a creature made at the end of the week's work when God was tired.

Mark Twain

254   He's a very sensitive man. He always closes his eyes when sitting on a train because he hates to see women standing.

255   I never said all actors are cattle, what I said was all actors should be treated like cattle.

Alfred Hitchcock

256   I find television very educating. Every time somebody turns on the set I go into the other room and read a book.

Groucho Marx

257   Two men were arguing in a restaurant about whether a third man across the room was the (Bishop of York). One man bet the other £50 that he was, and to settle the dispute went over to ask. He came back and said, 'We'll have to cancel the bet—he wouldn't tell me. In fact he told me to bugger off.'

258   He's a good boy; everything he steals he brings right home to mother.

Fred Allen

259 (If and only if you are *sure* you can handle long stories (and remember that very few people can) then the following is a classic. It has been around for years but is not often heard simply because it is not easy to tell well—be warned!)

A question is a physics exam asked, 'How would you determine the height of a building if you simply had a barometer?'

One student answered, 'Tie a piece of string to the end of the barometer, lower the barometer from the roof of the building to the ground; the length of the string, plus the length of the barometer, will equal the height of the building.'

The student was failed but he appealed to the university authorities on the ground that his answer was correct, and that he should have passed. An impartial arbiter ruled that although the answer was technically correct, it did not really display any knowledge of physics and he summoned the student and asked him to provide another answer.

'Well', said the student, 'you could drop the barometer off the roof and measure the time taken to reach the ground and work out the height of the building using the formula "height equals half times gravity-time squared".

'On the other hand, if the sun is shining, you could measure the height of the barometer, then set it up on end and measure the length of its shadow. Then use proportional arithmetic to work out the height of the building.

'If the building had an outside fire escape, you could simply walk up it and mark off the height of the skyscraper with a pencil, in barometer lengths, then add them up.

'Alternatively, you could measure the air-pressure on the roof using the barometer and compare it with standard air-pressure on the ground, then convert the difference in millibars into feet to give you the height.

'But the *simplest* way of all would be to knock on the security man's door and say, "If you will tell me the height of this building, I will give you this barometer." '

260   A bank is a place where they lend you an umbrella in fair weather and ask for it back again when it begins to rain.

Robert Frost

261   There comes a time to put aside principles . . . and do what's right.

262   How is that our memory is good enough to retain the least triviality that happens to us, and yet not good enough to recollect how often we have told it to the same person?

La Rochefoucauld

263   He's hoping to marry a rich woman who is too proud to let her husband work.

264   It usually takes me more than three weeks to prepare a good inpromptu speech.

Mark Twain

265   The only alliance I would make with the Women's Liberation Movement is in bed.

Abbie Hoffman

266   First man: 'Did you hear that 2,000 people went to the (referee's) funeral?'
Second man: 'Yes, it just goes to show, give the people what they want and . . .'

267   Most of us spend the first six days of each week sowing wild oats, then we go to church on Sunday and pray for a crop failure.

Fred Allen

268   No man in the world has more courage than the man who can stop after eating one peanut.

Channing Pollock

269   A Christian is a man who feels repentance on a Sunday for what he did on Saturday and is going to do on Monday.

Thomas R. Ybarra

270   She's very straight-laced. She still won't eat male jelly babies.

271   Every child should have an occasional pat on the back as long as it is applied low enough and hard enough.

Bishop Fulton J. Sheen

272   Clearly you were looking for a speaker who was elegant, witty and sophisticated but X (for example, an unsophisticated sportsman) couldn't come today because he had a fire at his house yesterday and his library burnt down. Both books were destroyed . . . which was a pity as he'd only coloured in one of them.

273   Against stupidity and vice-presidents the gods contend in vain.

Gregory Nunn

274   We are having the same old things for Christmas dinner this year . . . relatives.

275   Adam and Eve had many advantages, but the principal one was that they escaped teething.

Mark Twain

276   The thing that impresses me most about America is the way parents obey their children.

Duke of Windsor

277   Normally at dinner you have to make erudite conversation with one's neighbours. Obviously this isn't the case tonight.

278   Never keep up with the Joneses. Drag them down to your level. It's cheaper.

Quentin Crisp

279   A couple in their nineties consulted their solicitor about a divorce. He commented that they were rather old to be divorcing. They explained that they'd wanted to wait until their children were . . . dead.

280   Parents were invented to make children happy by giving them something to ignore.

Ogden Nash

281   On the subject of confused people, I liked the store detective who said he's seen a lot of people so confused that they'd stolen things, but never one so confused that they'd paid twice.

Baroness Phillips

282   When a friend commented that a man they both knew was always courteous to his inferiors, Dorothy Parker commented, 'Where does he find them?'

283   Try everything once except incest and folk-dancing.

Sir Thomas Beecham

284   As summer approaches we will soon hear that glorious sound of leather hitting . . . (name of appropriate batsman).

285   The only premarital thing girls don't do these days is cooking.

Omar Sharif

286   I'm not a great sportsman . . . although I did once hold the sponge at a rugby match.

287   Orators are most vehement when their cause is weak.

Cicero

288   The average girl would rather have beauty than brains because she knows that the average man can see much better than he can think.

Ladies' Home Journal

289   The public address people have now got equipment that will throw a speaker's voice half a mile. It's sometimes a pity that they haven't something that will throw speakers the same distance.

290   I went on a diet, swore off drinking and heavy eating, and in 14 days I lost two weeks.

Joe E. Lewis

291   A woman guest patted the large stomach of a man and said, 'If that was on a woman I'd know what it was.' He replied, 'Well, it was last night. What is it?'

292   Golf is so popular simply because it's the best game in the world at which to be bad.

A. A. Milne

293   An intellectual is a person educated beyond his intelligence.

Brandon Matthews

294   I never thought much of the courage of a lion-tamer. Inside the cage he is at least safe from people.

George Bernard Shaw

295   A psychiatrist is a fellow who asks you a lot of expensive questions your wife asks for nothing.

Joey Adams

296   Is sexual harassment at work a problem for the self-employed?

297   I've read the last page of the Bible. It's going to turn out all right.

Billy Graham

298   I've been privileged to see one of his school reports. Maths: he shows no aptitude whatsoever. English: the subject is beyond him. And so it went on. In his summary at the bottom the head had written, 'This is a considerable improvement on last time.'

299   To reform a man is tedious and uncertain labour; hanging is the sure work of a minute.

Douglas Jerrold

300   I went to a football match between the Ku Klux Klan and the Masons. I'm afraid the result must remain a secret.

301   Anybody who goes to see a psychiatrist ought to have his head examined.

Samuel Goldwyn

302   Privatization is going too far. I offered a £10 note to a toll collector at the [Dartford Tunnel] recently and he said 'Sold'.

303   They condemn what they do not understand.

Cicero

304   Hush, little bright line, don't you cry,
You'll be a cliché by and by.

Fred Allen

305   The hotel was so up-market that even room service was ex-directory.

306   A champion of the working man has never yet been known to die of overwork.

Robert Frost

307   Next to being witty yourself, the best thing is being able to quote another's wit.

Christian N. Bovee

308   Advertising agency: 85 per cent confusion and 15 per cent commission.

Fred Allen

309   Don't give a woman advice; one should never give a woman anything she can't wear in the evening.

Oscar Wilde

310   (Introducing soft dance music to a broadminded bunch) . . . and now we come to the erection section.

311   Ours is a world where people don't know what they want and are willing to go through hell to get it.

Don Marquis

312   You may be sure that when a man begins to call himself a 'realist', he is preparing to do something he is secretly ashamed of doing.

Sydney Harris

313   He's been worried recently because he's been getting threatening letters . . . from his bank manager.

314   Ignorance of the law must not prevent the losing lawyer from collecting his fee.

legal maxim

315   Women prefer men who have something tender about them—especially the legal kind.

Kay Ingram

316   Except for an occasional heart attack I feel as young as I ever did.

Robert Benchley

317   The only time he worries about obesity . . . is when he tries to spell it.

318   You have noticed that the less I know about a subject the more confidence I have; and the more light I throw on it.

Mark Twain

319   One of the first conditions of learning in a woman is to keep the fact a profound secret.

Honoré de Balzac

320   The efficiency of our criminal jury system is only marred by the difficulty of finding 12 men every day who don't know anything and can't read.

Mark Twain

321   The Iranians have unusual firing squads . . . they form circles.

322   My method is to take the utmost trouble to find the right thing to say, and then to say it with the utmost levity.

George Bernard Shaw

323   I know your guests enjoyed their meal, Mr Chairman. It's the first time I've seen people begin a meal with their elbows on starting blocks.

324   The boat was so old they started it with a whip.

325   Hanging is too good for a man who makes puns; he should be drawn and quoted.

Fred Allen

326   A pun is the lowest form of humour—when you don't think of it first.

Oscar Levant

327   Anybody can be good in the country.

Oscar Wilde

328   He missed a hole-in-one yesterday by . . . three strokes.

329   There's no trick to being a humorist when you have the whole government working for you.

Will Rogers

330   He is as good as his word—and his word is no good.

Seamus MacManus

331   If you are ever in doubt as to whether or not you should kiss a pretty girl, always give her the benefit of the doubt.

Thomas Carlyle.

332   Work is the refuge of people who have nothing better to do.

Oscar Wilde

333   The only time I went fishing, if the fish were biting, they must have been biting each other.

334   The noblest prospect which a Scotchman ever sees is the high road that leads him to England!

Samuel Johnson

335   It requires a surgical operation to get a joke well into a Scotch understanding.

Sydney Smith

336   Marriage is the miracle that transforms a kiss from a pleasure into a duty.

Helen Rowland

337   It was the sort of nightclub where you needed a heavy goods vehicle licence to dance with some of the girls.

338   First prize in the raffle is a 317-piece tea set. It was supposed to be 18-piece but the secretary dropped it.

339   If the Romans had been obliged to learn Latin they would never have found time to conquer the world.

Heinrich Heine

340   American women expect to find in their husbands a perfection that English women only hope to find in their butlers.

W. Somerset Maugham

341   I've met a few people in my time who were enthusiastic about hard work. And it was just my luck that all of them happened to be men I was working for at the time.

Bill Gold

342   The only place you can be sure of finding happiness is in the dictionary.

343   Women are like elephants to me; I like to look at them, but I wouldn't want to own one.

W. C. Fields

344   Many a man has fallen in love with a girl in a light so dim he would not have chosen a suit by it.

Maurice Chevalier

345   This evening has been everything I was led to expect . . .

346   Let's kill all the lawyers.

Shakespeare

347   Make love to every woman you meet; if you get five per cent on your outlays it's a good investment.

Arnold Bennett

348   Love doesn't make the world go round. Love is what makes the ride worth while.

Franklin P. Jones

349   The pay in the police force is good and the hours are reasonable. But the best part is that the customer is always wrong.

350   Eternal vigilance is the price of liberty.

John Philpot Curran

351   He's so cautious he put a roll-over bar on his speedboat.

352   Love is the word used to label the sexual excitement of the young, the habituation of the middle-aged, and the mutual dependence of the old.

John Ciardi

353   A VIP from a newly emerging country entered the dining room of the liner bringing him to Britain. He was very black and very large . . . and he had a sense of humour.

   He browsed through the menu for a while and then cried, 'There's nothing here that interests me. Let me see the passenger list.'

354 It matters not who won or lost . . . but how you placed the blame.

355 Everything comes to him who hustles while he waits.

Thomas A. Edison

356 Sexual intercourse is a grossly overrated pastime; the position is undignified, the pleasure momentary and the consequences utterly damnable.

Lord Chesterfield

357 He didn't want to leave any fingerprints so he wore mittens.

358 There is nothing so absurd that some philosopher has not already said.

Cicero

359 God heals, and the doctor takes the fee.

Franklin

360 'Twixt optimist and pessimist
The difference is droll—
The optimist sees the doughnut,
The pessimist the hole.

McLandburgh Wilson

361 I sometimes think that God in creating man somewhat over-estimated His ability.

Oscar Wilde

362 He's a very independent salesman—he takes orders from nobody.

363 It has to be admitted that we English have sex on the brain, which is a very unfortunate place to have it.

Malcolm Muggeridge

364 I only believe in striking children in self-defence.

365 Men who do not make advances to women are apt to become victims to women who make advances to them.

Walter Bagehot

366 The house is so rotten it only stands up because the woodworm hold hands.

367   The more extensive a man's knowledge of what has been done, the greater will be his power of knowing what to do.

Benjamin Disraeli

368   The only way to behave to a woman is to make love to her if she is pretty and to someone else if she is plain.

Oscar Wilde

369   People are not born bastards, they have to work at it.

Frank Dane

370   He is world famous . . . all over (small local town or area).

371   If only God would give me some clear sign! Like making a large deposit in my name at a Swiss bank.

Woody Allen

372   There are only two things I can't stand about him . . . his face.

373   A primitive artist is an amateur whose work sells.

Grandma Moses

374   They said I was a colourful boxer . . . black and blue.

375   Simple rules for saving money. To save half, when you are fired by an eager impulse to contribute to a charity, wait and count 40. To save three-quarters, count 60. To save it all, count 65.

Mark Twain

376   Don't mock the coffee. You may be old and weak yourself one day.

377   An autobigraphy usualy reveals nothing bad about its writer except his memory.

Franklin P. Jones.

378   Politicians (or any other group you wish to rib) are a bit like moneys . . . the higher they climb, the more they show their less desirable features.

379   The Bible tells us to love our neighbours, and also to love our enemies; probably because they are generally the same people.

G. K. Chesterton

380   The chef's special . . . but the food's terrible.

381   Put all your eggs in one basket and then watch that basket.

Mark Twain

382   I want everyone to tell me the truth, even if it costs him his job.

Sam Goldwyn

383   I want to be the white man's brother, not his brother-in-law.

Martin Luther King Jr

384   This won't be a long speech. I want to get through before the pills wear off.

385   France is a place where the money falls apart in your hands but you can't tear the toilet paper.

Billy Wilder

386   Some people read because they are too lazy to think.

G. C. Lichtenberg

387   He doesn't drink a lot . . . he spills most of it.

388   The louder he talked of his honour, the faster we counted our spoons.

Ralph Waldo Emerson

389   We need to finish fairly soon because on the stroke of midnight X (for example, the club secretary) turns into something ugly.

390   In the United States doing good has come to be, like patriotism, a favourite device of persons with something to sell.

H. L. Mencken

391   At a cricket function, run your hand along the carpet or tablecloth and say '(Club's leading bowler) has asked me to see if it will take spin.'

392   The emperor sent his troops to the field with immense enthusiasm; and he will lead them in person, when they return.

Mark Twain

393　X (manager of football club) is determined to get into Europe . . . even if he has to sing the blasted song himself (obviously can only be used if the Eurovision Song Contest survives).

394　The thing that takes up the least amount of time and causes the most amount of trouble is sex.

John Barrymore

395　No doubt Jack the Ripper excused himself on the grounds that it was human nature.

A. A. Milne

396　Rooms 7, 13, 56 and 28 are the numbers of adjacent rooms at the Belfast Hilton.

397　An archaeologist is the best husband any woman can have; the older she gets, the more interested he is in her.

Agatha Christie

398　They say see Naples and die. When you've seen X (town to be ribbed) it feels as if you already have.

399　He's finding it difficult to adapt to fame. He still has to ask autograph-hunters how to spell his name.

400　Few people think more than two or three times a year. I have made an international reputation for myself thinking once or twice a week.

George Bernard Shaw

401　There is one thing stronger than all the armies in the world: and that is an idea whose time has come.

Victor Hugo

402　They served haggis at the last dinner I attended. I didn't know whether to kick it or eat it. Having eaten it, I wished I'd kicked it.

403　I'm living so far beyond my income that we may almost be said to be living apart.

e e cummings

404 Nothing is so firmly believed as that which is least known.

Francis Jeffrey

405 In the old days newspaper proprietors used to send editors on world cruises if they were about to fire them. When one editor arrived back at Southampton he found the proprietor (who hadn't been able to find a suitable replacement) standing on the dock shouting 'Go round again.'

406 Occasionally, when honesty was the best policy, he was honest.

Gregory Nunn

407 She used to pose for centrefolds . . . in *Exchange & Mart*.

408 Each player in the band is a brilliant soloist. It's getting them to play together that's the problem.

409 An intellectual is a man who takes more words than necessary to tell more than he knows.

Dwight D. Eisenhower

410 Television is called a medium because anything good on it is rare.

Fred Allen

411 I know why most doctors don't smoke . . . they're usually too drunk to light the damn things.

412 The American arrives in Paris with a few French phrases he has culled from a conversational guide or picked up from a friend who owns a beret.

Fred Allen

413 As he intoned the Ten Commandments, the priest was surprised to see a man slip out as he got to 'Thou shalt not commit adultery.' The man apologized later and explained that he'd just remembered where he'd left his umbrella.

414 In the theatre there is comedy and tragedy. If the house is packed it's a comedy, otherwise it's a tragedy.

Sol Hurok

415   He's the sort of man who feeds stray puppies . . . to piranha fish.

416   The soup is never hot enough if the waiter can keep his thumb in it.

William Collier

417   The last venue I spoke in was so scruffy that vandals broke in and decorated it.

418   He who hesitates is last.

Mae West

419   Lecturing about a remote island, a professor said that it had a surplus of men and that 'even women as plain as those here today would easily find husbands.'
   Not unnaturally all the female students started to walk out in protest, at which the professor shouted, 'Don't rush, there isn't a plane for another three days.'

420   (If you have to attend a Burns supper and the ceremonies drag on—they will—you *may* risk saying) 'I've read of people suffering from burns. Now I know how they feel.'

421   Laws are spider webs through which the big flies pass and the little ones get caught.

Honoré de Balzac

422   A minister of the old school was in full song and flailing at his congregation, 'And, yes, there will be much weeping and gnashing of teeth.'
   One elderly parishioner, with no teeth, relaxed and closed his eyes. He was awoken by the cry, 'Don't kid yourself, McTavish. Teeth will be provided.'

423   The minute you read something you can't understand, you can almost be sure it was drawn up by a lawyer.

Will Rogers

424   Nowadays a man is known by the company he owns.

425   He talks with more claret than clarity.

426 When flying, I never worry about how the engines are mounted. What the fitters do behind closed hangar doors is their business.

427 I think the light at the end of the economic tunnel is starting to flicker again.

428 A diplomat is a man who always remembers a woman's birthday but never remembers her age.

Robert Frost

429 She likes macho men—she even gave her husband a Harris tweed apron for his birthday.

430 I looked myself up in *Who's Who* . . . but I'm not in it.

431 No grand idea was ever born in a conference, but a lot of foolish ideas have died there.

F. Scott Fitzgerald

432 He's so fat he had to stop playing cricket because every time he was hit on the backside the umpire gave a wide.

433 Whenever he photographs lawyers or accountants he always says, 'Say "fees".'

434 Give your decisions, never your reasons; your decisions may be right, your reasons are sure to be wrong.

Earl of Mansfield

435 If you tell people a star is so many million miles away, they will believe you. Put a sign saying 'wet paint' and they feel an irresistible urge to touch and check.

436 The first essential of leadership is to get a bunch of dumb idiots to follow you.

437 At least I have the modesty to admit that lack of modesty is one of my failings

Hector Berlioz

438 A dog owner called a vet at midnight to say his pedigree dog had been mounted by a neighbour's mongrel. The vet said 'Throw a bucket of water over them

or hit them with a stick.' The owner said he tried and
neither had worked.

The vet then said 'Well, put the phone down near the
dogs and I'll call you back.'

Owner: 'Will that stop them?'

Vet: 'Well, it worked here.'

439   He's the only man I know who has sent a suit to the
dry-cleaner's . . . with a blanket in each pocket.

440   I wonder whether what we are publishing now is
worth cutting down trees to make paper for the stuff.

Richard Brautigan

441   He's so short-sighted that when we sent a rescue
helicopter for him, he threw bread for it.

442   Jesus wasn't from here . . . because they couldn't
find three wise men or a virgin.

443   I suppose it is much more comfortable to be mad and
not know it, than to be sane and have one's doubts.

G. B. Burgin

444   When she played the part of Lady Godiva, people
looked at the horse.

445   I think women do have equality today. I was only
saying so to my wife this morning as she was cleaning my
shoes.

446   When I whispered an improper suggestion to the car
saleslady, she grinned and said 'You got that when you
bought the car from us.'

447   Statistics are like a bikini. What they reveal is
suggestive, but what they conceal is vital.

Aaron Levenstein

448   When he saw your chairman in evening dress, David
Attenborough was all for mounting another expedition.

449   Well, this is the moment you've all been waiting for
. . . and there it goes.

450   I play golf in the low 80s. If it's any hotter than that, I won't play.

Joe E. Lewis

451   Your chairman asked if I believed in free speech. I said of course I did—it's fundamental to our democracy. He said 'Good, can you make one on (date)?'

452   He is, of course, a graduate of the (politician or businessman in the news for sharpness) School of Charm and Diplomacy.

453   Whom the gods wish to destroy they first call promising.

Cyril Connolly

454   He bows his head every Sunday morning. He really *must* keep his eye on the ball.

455   After an interminable lecture, the professor concluded 'And so we prove that X equals nought.'
Student: 'To think we did all that for nothing.'

456   When choosing between two evils, I always like to try the one I've never tried before.

Mae West

457   Liberty means responsibility. That is why most men dread it.

George Bernard Shaw

458   This is a wonderful place to come . . . from.

459   There is nothing so nice as doing good by stealth and being found out by accident.

Charles Lamb

460   He's sold me an interesting assurance policy. If I get to 65 I will be able to live in luxury until I'm . . . 66. If I die earlier I have to pay a small fine.

461   Nothing is more admirable than the fortitude with which millionaires tolerate the disadvantage of their wealth.

Rex Stout

462   Driving certainly causes stress. Yesterday I hammered on the roof of a car in a traffic jam . . . I wouldn't normally do that to a nun in broad daylight.

463   I was approached by someone who wanted political asylum so I directed them to the House of Commons.

464   Too many people are thinking of security instead of opportunity. They seem more afraid of life than death.

James F. Byrnes

465   I sat next to a Frenchman at a dinner and when a fly landed on my plate I said, 'Regardez le mouche.' The Frenchman said, 'Non, non: *la* mouche,' and explained that 'fly' is feminine. I didn't realize the French had such incredible eyesight.

466   (If they are running sweeps on the length of speeches)
Your chairman says such sweeps are illegal under the Lotteries and Amusements Act . . . but has asked me to speak for exactly 13 minutes.

467   If I break wind in Wurttenberg they smell it in Rome.

Martin Luther

468   He thinks Hertz Van Rental is a Dutch Impressionist painter.

469   If I have been able to see farther than others, it was because I stood on the shoulders of giants.

Sir Isaac Newton

470   He flew 12 successful missions as a kamikaze pilot.

471   His five-year-old got a part in the school play as a man who'd been married 25 years. If he's good they say he can have a speaking part next time.

472   The only think I like about rich people is their money.

Lady Astor

473   He helps old ladies . . . half-way across the road.

474   He was a strange child. He used to collect cigarette cards of famous taxidermists.

475   A converted cannibal is one who, on Friday, eats only fishermen.

Emily Lotney

476   (If waiters or guests move about as you are speaking) Are you on a sponsored walk?

477   (If there is a lot of noise) I think they are trying to train me as a police horse.

478   I don't care what is written about me as long as it isn't true.

Katherine Hepburn

479   He does the work of two men . . . Laurel and Hardy.

480   He owes a lot to (the association). He owes a lot to the [NatWest] too.

481   Millions long for immortality who do not know what to do with themselves on a rainy Sunday afternoon.

Susan Ertz

482   Typical British tourists—matching suitcases . . . and three carrier bags.

483   The sun never sets on the (people to be ribbed). They say it's because God doesn't trust them in the dark.

484   I could tell he was at the office when he phoned . . . I could hear his secretary shouting, 'Drink up.'

485   Flying first class is a bit like being in hospital—they wake you up every few hours to give you orange juice.

486   The superior man understands what is right; the inferior man understands what will sell.

Confucius

487   A message for all ships in the (inland town) area . . . clear off—there's no water.

488   She had long black curly hair . . . on her legs.

489   A thing is not necessarily true because a man dies for it.

Oscar Wilde

490   He's a maniakleptic . . . he keeps backing into shops and leaving things.

491   The audience was so old its walking sticks were deemed to constitute a fire hazard.

492   A liberal is a person whose interests aren't at stake at the moment.

Willis Player

493   The area is so rough even the Alsatians go around in pairs.

494   Having flown by X (airline) I can appreciate why the Pope always kisses the tarmac when he lands.

495   Advertising is the rattling of a stick inside a swill bucket.

George Orwell

496   It's the first time I've spoken in an aircraft hangar (or furniture warehouse or X's front room).

497   Britain can't be finished if it is capable of developing such a major contribution to the space programme as . . . the heat-seeking suppository.

498   Nature, not content with denying him the ability to think, has endowed him with the ability to write.

A. E. Housman

499   If he is asked to count up to 21 he gets done for indecent exposure.

500   It is always the best policy to speak the truth, unless, of course, you are an exceptionally good liar.

Jerome K. Jerome

501   He's so haughty he won't even travel in the same car as his chauffeur.

502   Now there's an Anglers Anonymous. Phone them up and they let you tell them a pack of lies.

503   Nowadays people treat the Ten Commandments like a history exam . . . they only attempt three.

504   He has every attribute of a dog except loyalty.

Senator Thomas P. Gore

505   The Chairman of the Scottish Tourist Board saw him in a swimsuit . . . and has asked him to spend next summer swimming up and down Loch Ness.

506   An engineer had been invited to address you tonight but, sadly, couldn't find his way here because, like many engineers, he is numerate but not literate. So when he gets to a signpost he knows how far it is . . . but not where to.

507   I saw a gravestone saying, 'Here lies a [lawyer] and an honest man.' I didn't realize they were burying people two to a grave.

508   Good taste and humour are a contradiction in terms, like a chaste whore.

Malcolm Muggeridge

509   We plan to have a trip to Madame Tussaud's and (HQ of association) with prizes for those who can guess which is which.

510   Tact is the art of making a point without making an enemy.

Howard W. Newton

511   This is one of the best 10 hotels in (name of street or village).

512   I've flown 480 hours with X (airline) . . . 39 of them in the air.

513   He's so macho he uses [Black and Decker] after-shave.

514   Fashion is a form of ugliness so intolerable that we have to alter it every six months.

515   If you fly tourist class it makes you very Christian—the seats are so tight that you simply *have* to turn the other cheek.

516   The most dangerous food a man can eat is his wedding cake.

517 He's always prepared to lend a hand to those . . . above him.

518 Lame ducks quack a lot, but they seldom get off the ground.

519 Since we have to speak well of the dead, let's knock them while they're alive.

John Sloan

520 I'm not afraid to die. I just don't want to be there when it happens.

Woody Allen

521 I know I shouldn't name-drop. Prince Charles was telling me about it only the other day.

522 Women are made to be loved, not understood.

Oscar Wilde

523 As the woman lay on the couch awaiting artificial insemination, the doctor came in with his trousers over his arm and said: 'I'm sorry, we've no more bottles—you'll have to have draught.'

524 Tact is the ability to describe others as they see themselves.

Abraham Lincoln

525 Marriage has many pains but celibacy has no pleasures.

Samuel Johnson

526 It's said he wears Tupperware underpants . . . to keep everything nice and fresh.

527 Every production of genius must be the production of enthusiasm.

Benjamin Disraeli

528 Cribbing always seems to me to be making the best use of available resources.

529 The whole strength of England lies in the fact that the enormous majority of English people are snobs.

George Bernard Shaw

530   First man: 'It looks as if we're about to be mugged.'
Second man: 'Here's the £5 I owe you.'

531   If a playwright is funny, the English look for a
serious message, and if he's serious, they look for a joke.

Sacha Guitry

532   I've got to the age when I need my false teeth and
my hearing aid before I can ask where I've left my glasses.

533   Bad officials are elected by good citizens who do not
vote.

534   (Different professions present at a function can be
grouped as follows)
A doctor, an architect and a politician were arguing over
whose was the oldest profession. The doctor said that as
Eve was made from Adam's rib that implied medical skills.
The architect argued that before Adam and Eve order was
created out of chaos which was clearly an architectural
task.
'True', agreed the politican, 'but who do you think created
the chaos in the first place?'

535   Most people have some sort of religion. At least they
know which church they're staying away from.

John Erskine

536   Friends. Well, I feel I know you too well to call you
ladies and gentlemen.

537   Of all sexual aberrations, chastity is the strangest.

Anatole France

538   It was a real battle of wits. How brave of him to go
into battle unarmed.

539   If you think before you speak, the other fellow gets
his joke in first.

Ed Howe

540   He wanted to play hide and seek as a child . . . but
no-one would look for him.

541   The pilot asked how high we wanted to fly. We said 33 inches because we knew it was his inside leg measurement.

542   Never tell the truth to a pimp, a whore, or a corporate vice-president.

Frank Dane

543   The only success our football team had was when the Pools Panel picked it for a home win.

544   When we hang the capitalists they will sell us the rope we use.

Joseph Stalin

545   He's so rich he's had to hire the Grand Canyon . . . as a petty cash box.

546   The best government is a benevolent tyranny tempered by an occasional assassination.

Voltaire

547   As part of the medical he had to weigh himself in the nude. But he's refused to do it again . . . he found it very embarrassing in Boots.

548   At a function like this recently I sat next to a vision of loveliness in a purple dress, and when the music started I asked if I could have the first dance.
   The vision said, 'I'm sorry but there are three reasons why I can't dance with you. This is a banquet not a ball; they are playing the Austrian national anthem . . . and I'm the Archbishop of Salzburg.'

549   The ideal love affair is one conducted by post.

550   What can I say that hasn't already been said about (someone currently unpopular)?

551   Insurance is always a problem. Pianists insure their hands and singers insure their voices. Even male ballet dancers have to be insured for a lump sum.

552   It is an old maxim of mine that when you have excluded the imposible, whatever remains, however improbable, must be the truth.

Sir Arthur Conan Doyle

553 When charged with gross indecency he complained that he's only done it 143 times.

554 All the world loves a lover, but not while the love-making is going on.

Elbert Hubbard

555 The indoor athletic meeting has had to be cancelled . . . because it's a nice day.

556 Though the mills of God grind slowly, yet they
grind exceeding small;
Though with patience He stands waiting, with
exactness grinds He all.

Friedrich von Logau

557 He captained the school fencing team . . . until they ran out of creosote.

558 Like the measles, love is most dangerous when it comes late in life.

Lord Byron

559 He's been asked to pose nude for the centrefold of *Playgirl* magazine next month and there'll be a free gift for all the readers . . . a magnifier.

560 He's very cautious. At home he won't leave the landing light on in case a plane crashes on to the roof.

561 War is too important to be left to the generals.

Georges Clemenceau

562 A girl was washed up on a desert island and found a lonely man there who'd been marooned for 20 years. She asked him what he did for food and he explained that he got water out of the lagoon and, mostly, he dug for clams. She then asked him what he did for sex and he said he'd been on the island for so long he didn't know what she meant. She showed him and then asked how he felt.
Man: 'Fine—but look what you've done to my clam digger.'

563 No man is fit to be called a sportsman that doesn't kick his wife out of bed an average of once every three weeks.

Robert Smith Surtrees

564   Women must make better soldiers than men because you never hear *them* coughing when they take a medical.

565   The sight of a drunkard is a better sermon against that vice than the best that was ever preached on that subject.

Saville

566   He was asked by the police to help with an identity parade. Two night-club hostesses walked along the line and picked him out. I must stress that he was completely innocent . . . but when he heard what he was charged with he was so proud that he pleaded guilty.

567   The trouble with being tolerant is that people think you don't understand the problem.

Merle L. Meacham

568   He said it was a matter of life and death. It turned out he was an insurance salesman.

569   Most people would rather defend to the death your right to say it than listen to it.

Robert Brault

570   When the head waiter here died they put on his gravestone 'God finally caught his eye.'

571   The fastest way for a poltician to become an elder statesman is to lose an election.

Earl Wilson

572   I asked your secretary how many men would be present, how many women, and how old you'd be. In market research terms I asked if you were broken down by age and sex. He said he thought most of you are.

573   I didn't like the play, but then I saw it under adverse conditions—the curtain was up.

Groucho Marx

574   My wife adores children and spends most of her time with them . . . that's why she cut up your chairman's steak tonight.

575 An expert is one who knows more and more about less and less.

Nicholas Murray Butler

576 He got his bride to wear a nightgown made of 100 yards of nun's veiling. He loves a good fumble.

577 Her husband made her happy by adding some magic to their marriage . . . he disappeared.

578 He thinks things through very clearly before going off half-cocked.

General Carl Spaatz

579 He asked for three cups of coffee in his flask . . . one without sugar.

580 In politics nothing is contemptible.

Benjamin Disraeli

581 Buy old masters. They fetch a much better price than old mistresses.

Lord Beaverbrook

582 My doctor keeps giving me tablets that are good for asthma. I wish he'd give me something that's *bad* for it.

583 A hair in the head is worth two in the brush.

Oliver Herford

584 You can tell he's *nouveau riche*—he still spits on his hands before swinging his golf club.

585 The desire for safety stands against every great and noble enterprise.

Tacitus

586 Modern houses are so small we've had to train our dog to wag its tail up and down and not sideways.

587 Mother always said that honesty was the best policy, and money isn't everything. She was wrong about other things too.

Gerald Barzan

588 I wouldn't say he's mean but he keeps his money in his right-hand pocket . . . and he's left-handed.

589   A celebrity is a person who works hard all his life to become well known, and then wears dark glasses to avoid being recognized.

Fred Allen

590   A speech is like a love affair. Any fool can start it, but to end it requires considerable skill.

Lord Mancroft

591   Censorship ends in logical completeness when nobody is allowed to read any books except the books nobody reads.

George Bernard Shaw

592   There may be some things better than sex, and some things may be worse. But there is nothing exactly like it.

W. C. Fields

593   Men of few words are the best men.

Shakespeare

594   I understand medical research scientists are now using X (for example, lawyers) instead of mice for their experiments . . . there are more of them and you don't get so attached to them.

595   He only passed exams in scripture and woodwork. If fact for a time it looked as if he would become an undertaker.

596   Contrary to popular belief, English women do not wear tweed nightgowns.

Hermione Gingold

597   At school they soon noticed his early lack of promise.

598   I didn't hear all the boss said . . . I was on my knees at the time.

599   Men occasionally stumble over the truth, but most of them pick themselves up and hurry off as if nothing had happened.

Winston Churchill

600 Our dog chases people on a bike. We've had to take it off him.

601 In England I would rather be a man, a horse, a dog or a woman, in that order. In America I think the order would be reversed.

Bruce Gould

602 The place is so up-market even the fire brigade is ex-directory.

603 I applied for a job as a disc-jockey but when I admitted I could read and write they said I was over-qualified.

604 Magellan went around the world in 1521—which isn't too many strokes when you consider the distance.

Joe Laurie, Jr

605 When he got the 'flu the doctor told him to avoid crowds, so he spent the time in (rival's showroom).

606 An Englishman is a creature who thinks he is being virtuous when he is only being uncomfortable.

George Bernard Shaw

607 God equipped us with necks—we should occasionally stick them out.

608 If there is anything a public servant hates to do it's something for the public.

Kim Hubbard

609 He got things off to a flying stop.

610 We learn from experience. A man never wakes up his second baby just to see it smile.

Grace Williams

611 The men call the foreman 'Balloons' because he keeps saying, 'Don't let me down lads.'

612 If at first you don't succeed, try, try again. Then quit. There's no use being a damn fool about it.

W. C. Fields

613 If women do what efficiency experts do, it's called nagging.

614 I've read some of your modern free verse and wonder who set it free.

John Barrymore

615 The bride looked stunning; the groom looked stunned.

616 With an evening coat and a white tie, anybody, even a stockbroker, can gain a reputation for being civilized.

Oscar Wilde

617 The raffle prizes were so rotten, the winners wouldn't own up.

618 Love thy neighbour as thyself, but choose your neighbourhood.

Louise Beal

619 A rich man asked his girlfriend if she would still love him if he lost all his money. 'Of course sweetheart . . . but I'd miss you.'

620 He irritates his wife because he *doesn't* talk in his sleep . . . he just grins.

621 If sex is such a natural phenomenon, how come there are so many books on how to?

Bette Midler

622 A differential is if I earn more than you. An anomaly is if you get more than me.

623 At the end of the evening we'll have a singsong to some old HMV records but please only sing for *exactly* 3½ minutes and then stop . . . otherwise the needle scratches the dog's backside.

624 He has a wonderful war record . . . Vera Lynn singing 'We'll meet again'.

625 God will forgive me; that's his business.

Heinrich Heine

626 I'm not sure if the cheese we had was imported or deported from France.

627 People will buy anything that's one to a customer.

Sinclair Lewis

628 I'm delighted to announce he's just got a TV contract . . . £50 down and £5 per month.

629 I was asked to propose a toast to absent friends . . . so I coupled it with the name of the wine waiter.

630 That which seems the height of absurdity in one generation often becomes the height of wisdom in another.

Adlai Stevenson

631 He's taken so many iron tablets, he swivels round in bed until he's facing north.

632 An honest politican is one who, when he's bought, stays bought.

Simon Cameron

633 I was never a good cricketer, although I was once in a position to shout 'wait'.

634 I distrust camels, and anyone else who can go a week without a drink.

Joe E. Lewis

635 He took her out to a Chinese restaurant for a romantic meal and asked 'How would you like your rice, boiled or fried?' She gazed at him and said 'Thrown.'

636 She's descended from a long line her mother listened to.

Gypsy Rose Lee

637 He is so well built he had the name of that Welsh railway station tatooed in a very intimate place. You know the place—Rhyl.

638 It is the patriotic duty of every man to lie for his country.

Alfred Adler

639 I thought the choice of Peruvian claret for the top table was particularly inspired.

640 They've introduced a marvellous incentive scheme: if at first you don't succeed, you're fired.

641 He took the job fired with enthusiasm. Three months later he left the same way.

642 Democracy means government by the uneducated, while aristocracy means government by the badly educated.

G. K. Chesterton

643 He hired what he thought was a spicy video about three in a bed. It turned out to be about darts.

644 I wasn't a bit nervous during the landing . . . the plane finished up yards from the edge of the cliff.

645 He's even had a rose named after him. No good in beds but good against walls.

646 He doesn't know the meaning of the word despair. He doesn't know the meaning of a lot of other words either.

647 We can't all be heroes because someone has to sit on the curb and clap as they go by.

Will Rogers

648 He bought a drink and we sat . . . sharing this lager.

649 The majority of us are for free speech only when it deals with those subjects concerning which we have no intense conviction.

Edmund B. Chaffee

650 The PR department keeps me on such a tight rein, I'm not even allowed to say 'no comment.'

651 We went to a wife-swapping party where we threw our keys into the middle . . . I drew an AA box.

652 I'm sorry I'm late. The lift said 'Six people only' so I had to wait for five more.

653 We know no spectacle so ridiculous as the British public in one of its periodical fits of morality.

Thomas Babington Macaulay

654 We have electronic equipment at work which can do the work of three executives . . . or one secretary.

655 He was late because he had to go round the roundabout 15 times—his indicator was stuck.

656 If you think women are the weaker sex . . . try pulling the sheets back to your side.

657 He's the kind of man who picks his friends—to pieces.

Mae West

658 I picked up a hitchhiker on the way here. It was only fair I suppose as I'd knocked him down in the first place.

659 Medicine is a collection of uncertain prescriptions, the results of which, taken collectively, are more fatal than useful to mankind.

Napoleon Bonaparte

660 They say a speech is a bit like visiting a nudist camp: the first couple of minutes are the hardest.

661 I don't like to commit myself about heaven and hell—you see, I have friends in both places.

Mark Twain

662 Good news for X (airline): Glen Miller's plane has finally landed in Paris.

663 Misers aren't fun to live with, but they make wonderful ancestors.

David Brenner

664 She went on the streets but after the first evening she was 45p down.

665 He was a fine friend. He stabs you in the front.

Leonard Louis Levinson

666 He holds the record at Brands Hatch for pit stops: nine in a ten-lap race. One for tyres and eight to ask the way.

667 When he was charged with an indecent act at Beechers Brook, he asked for 20 other fences to be taken into consideration.

668   If England treats her criminals the way she has treated me, she doesn't deserve to have any.

Oscar Wilde

669   The only time I ever boxed, I took one punch . . . and had to pay to get back into the hall.

670   It is unfair to believe everything we hear about lawyers—some of it might not be true.

Gerald F. Lieberman

671   Her first meal for him was rhubarb pie; it was 12 inches long and 1 inch thick.

672   When I came back to Dublin I was court-martialled in my absence and sentenced to death in my absence, so I said they could shoot me in my absence.

Brendan Behan

673   He thought the Walls of Jericho was an Israeli ice-cream factory.

674   My notion of a wife at 40 is that a man should be able to change her, like a bank note, for two 20s.

Douglas Jerrold

675   I asked her why she didn't tell me when she had an orgasm. She said, 'Because you're never there.'

676   The long and distressing controversy over capital punishment is very unfair to anyone meditating murder.

Geoffrey Fisher

677   There were so few there that they asked if I could run the audience home.

678   Ignorance of the law excuses no man from practicing it.

Addison Mizner

679   I've got a soft spot for X. A bog in Ireland.

680   We've just had the results of the (Irish) sheepdog trials . . . 12 have been found guilty.

681   He's been given pills to take to increase his strength . . . but he can't get the top off the bottle.

682   I'm so unlucky that when I went on the hobbyhorse at a fairground . . . I got four faults.

683   A coward is a hero with a wife, kids, and a mortgage.

Marvin Kitman

684   It's good to see that he is still modelling for toby jugs.

685   A husband should tell his wife everything that he is sure she will find out.

Thomas R. Dewar

686   When he changes a £20 note he gets everyone to sing 'Auld Lang Syne'.

687   The trouble with her is that she lacks the power of conversation but not the power of speech.

George Bernard Shaw

688   His parents gave him an unusual rattle as a baby . . . there was a snake on the other end.

689   If there are any tax inspectors here, the manager's asked me to point out that they're not usually this busy.

690   Later there'll be a contest when you have to guess the chef's real job.

691   A husband and wife who have separate bedrooms have either drifted apart or found happiness.

Honoré de Balzac

692   Please raise your hands if you have finished listening so that I know who I'm still addressing.

693   He's got his dog trained so that it only does it on newspapers. The trouble is it does it when he's reading the blasted things.

694   When people are free to do as they please, they usually imitate each other.

Eric Hoffer

695   She was wearing the kind of dress you can see through . . . but don't want to.

696   When I got measles as a child, my parents fought for my right to die.

697   Music played at weddings always reminds me of the music played for soldiers before they go into battle.

Heinrich Heine

698   When you retire from the company you have to turn in your ulcers.

699   If an opera cannot be played by an organ-grinder, it is not going to achieve immortality.

Sir Thomas Beecham

700   So, will you please raise your glasses . . . of cheap wine.

701   Second   marriage: the   triumph   of   hope   over experience.

Samuel Johnson

702   (After a joke flops)
And some fell on stony ground.

703   Isn't technology wonderful? Have you noticed if you stop at traffic lights and they turn green, that immediately activates the horn of the car behind.

704   He may be at the top of the tree—but he's not a fairy by any means.

705   People who say they sleep like a baby usually don't have one.

Leo J. Burke

706   I couldn't blame him for reversing into me, I suppose—he couldn't see for his 'child on board' stickers.

707   It's a big day here tomorrow . . . the chef's going to wash his hands.

708   Marriage is popular because it combines the maximum of temptation with the maximum of opportunity.

George Bernard Shaw

709   I asked her to take her veil off so that I could kiss her. It was unfortunate that she wasn't wearing one.

710 A little sincerity is a dangerous thing, and a great deal of it is absolutely fatal.

Oscar Wilde

711 The food is so bad that pygmies come here to dip their arrows in the soup.

712 Any intelligent woman who reads the marriage contract, and then goes into it, deserves all the consequences.

Isadora Duncan

713 The band have been requested to play (any popular tune). They don't know it but they're going to play one which uses many of the same notes.

714 You can be sincere and still be stupid.

Charles F. Kettering

715 They wouldn't give this spot to a leopard.

716 Never argue at the dinner table, for the one who is not hungry always gets the best of the argument.

Richard Whately

717 They told me to bring something to drink . . . so I brought your chairman.

718 They made love as though they were an endangered species.

Peter de Vries

719 They even make him march at the back at demos.

720 So much of what we call management consists in making it difficult for people to work.

Peter Drucker

721 (If people on a top table are wearing regalia) I feel as if I'm on a chain gang.

722 You will be relieved to hear that I do not intend to use the full two hours allotted to me.

723 The English instinctively admire any man who has no talent and is modest about it.

James Agee

724 I don't think anything can compare with the church's new advertising campaign—I stopped at a crossroads outside a cemetery and a large sign read 'Do not enter the box until your exit is clear.'

725 Where would we be without our wives? Gleneagles?

726 (If a hot venue)
If you see a dragonfly, don't kill it—it's part of the computer-controlled air conditioning.

727 Man is the only animal that blushes. Or needs to.

Mark Twain

728 He's always been a bit of a rebel . . . he even eats After Eight mints at 7.30.

729 I would rather be an opportunist and float than go to the bottom with my principles round my neck.

Stanley Baldwin

730 He has a clear sense of priorities. He was asked to be an usher at a wedding and when the groom, after being reassured about the cars and the choir, asked about the bells, he said, 'It's OK—I've ordered four crates of it.'

731 Breathes there a man with hide so tough
Who says two sexes aren't enough?

Samuel Hoffenstein

732 Welsh choirmaster after a rousing rendition of 'John Peel': 'Beautiful, beautiful but Blodwyn, it was the sound of his horn roused her from his bed . . . not the size of it.'

733 My neighbours had a letter from their daughter away at boarding school which said, 'Dear both, You may remember I wrote to tell you that the school had caught fire. What I didn't tell you was that I was rescued by a handsome fireman and, to cut a long story short, I've left school and am sharing a caravan with him and his three young children, his wife having walked out. And now I think I'm pregnant. Love Margaret. P.S. None of the above is true but I think I've failed my exams and it's high time the family got its priorities sorted out.'

734   Every woman is wrong until she cries, and then she is right; instantly.

Sam Slick

735   I'm the only one on the top table I've never heard of.

736   It is a horrible, demoralizing thing to be a lawyer. You look for such low motives in everyone and everything.

Katherine T. Hinkson

737   When I got the invitation to speak, I didn't hesitate . . . I said 'no'.

738   Teaching is the fine art of imparting knowledge without possessing it.

Mark Twain

739   I had a terrible dream—(Raquel Welch) and (Mrs Thatcher) were fighting over me . . . and (Mrs Thatcher) was winning.

740   I know only two tunes: one of them is 'Yankee Doodle' and the other isn't.

Ulysees S. Grant

741   When X took over it's no exaggeration that we stood on the edge of a precipice. Under his leadership of course we've taken a giant step forward.

742   Wagner had some wonderful moments but awful half-hours.

Gioacchino Rossini

743   He's known as a dynamo . . . because everything he does is charged up.

744   The audience was reserved and quietly attentive— until Rita Hayworth danced on to the screen in a flaming red dress, cut to show a major part of her acting ability.

Gerald F. Lieberman

745   He's never gone to bed with an ugly woman. Mind, he's woken up with a few.

746   The first Rotarian was the first man to call John the Baptist, Jack.

H. L. Mencken

747   Even the fax machine has ulcers.

748   His full name is John 'Damn' Smith . . . because the vicar stubbed his toe during the christening.

749   When you go to drown yourself always take off your clothes, they may fit your wife's next husband.

Gregory Nunn

750   He was educated at Oxford . . . one Wednesday afternoon.

751   A nation is a society united by a delusion about its ancestry and by a common hatred of its neighbours.

Dean William R. Inge

752   He is a man of many parts . . . most of which you can't get any more.

753   Maybe this world is another planet's hell.

Aldous Huxley

754   Will the owner of the orange Cortina with the black striped seat covers and 'Sharon and Kevin' over the top of the windscreen please make himself known to the hotel manager? There's nothing the matter with your car—he just wants to see what you look like.

755   The best way to get on in the world is to make people believe it's to their advantage to help you.

Jean de la Bruyère

756   I wouldn't say he's mean, but his favourite drink is whisky and Horlicks—which ensures he's asleep when it's his turn to buy a round.

757   I refuse to admit I'm more than 52 even if that does make my sons illegitimate.

Lady Astor

758   His wife keeps her eyes closed when they make love—she hates to see him enjoy himself.

759   A successful lawsuit is one worn by a policeman.

Robert Frost

760 He earns so much he puts an X on his pay packet to indicate he doesn't want any publicity.

761 She's the kind of woman who climbed the ladder of success—wrong by wrong.

Mae West

762 He was really enjoying himself on the flight home, in fact he arrived back 20 minutes after the plane.

763 He's got one of those time-saving video recorders—it plays programmes back while you are out.

764 When a man retires and time is no longer a matter of urgent importance, his colleages generally present him with a watch.

R. C. Sherriff

765 A professor saw a beautiful girl at a party and said, 'I remember you—Course 3, Thursday 18 March, row F, seat 3.'
Girl: 'Yes, I was there. But who are you?'

766 As lousy as things are now, tomorrow they will be somebody's good old days.

Gerald Barzan

767 I asked my wife where she'd like to go for a second honeymoon. She said Lourdes.

768 First you forget names, then you forget faces, then you forget to pull your zipper up, then you forget to pull your zipper down.

Leo Rosenberg

769 It's such a rough area there's a six-month waiting list to vandalize a phone box.

770 We operate on trust and understanding. They don't trust us and we don't understand them.

771 When science discovers the centre of the universe a lot of people will be disappointed to find they are not it.

Bernard Baily

772 He always lands . . . on other people's feet.

773   I noticed it was 7 p.m. for 7.30. The functions I speak at are usually 7.44 for 7.45 and buy your own drinks.

774   I'd have had more success as a cricketer but the captain persisted in sending me in in the middle of hat-tricks.

775   Some movie stars wear their sunglasses even in church. They're afraid God might not recognize them and ask for autographs.

Fred Allen

776   The first prize in the raffle will be a Marcel Marceau LP.

777   I know you haven't heard of me in (place where speaking). I usually speak in (town further away). Mind, they haven't heard of me there either.

778   No man can be a pure specialist without being in the strict sense an idiot.

George Bernard Shaw

779   He's had trouble with his car . . . the credit company repossessed it.

780   He was charged with breaking into a £10 note . . . but the police released him when they realized it was a first offence.

781   He took his car for its first service . . . but got it jammed in the doors of the church.

782   We all worry about the population explosion—but we don't worry about it at the right time.

Arthur Hoppe

783   Finally, as a tribute to all Americans, we will sing 'Yank my Doodle—it's a Dandy.'

784   He was told his girlfriend was pregnant and asked what steps he planned to take.
Answer: 'Big ones.'

785   Children should never discuss sex in the presence of their elders.

Gregory Nunn

786 It was a society wedding . . . we held it at the Co-op.

787 The pen is mightier than the sword! The case for prescriptions rather than surgery.

Marvin Kitman

788 It's a change to find my name in bigger type than the soup.

789 It's useless to hold a person to anything he says while he's in love, drunk, or running for office.

Shirley MacLaine

790 After he appeared in a Shakespearean play at school, the local newspaper wrote, 'Some parents had already seen X as Hamlet . . . but they laughed just the same.'

791 One must have a heart of stone to read the death of Little Nell without laughing.

Oscar Wilde

792 You can always tell readers of X (magazine or newspaper). They move their lips when they read.

793 When the insects take over the world we hope they will remember, with gratitude, how we took them along on all our picnics.

Bill Vaughn

794 When he was kidnapped his parents sprang into action . . . they rented out his room.

795 When the military man approaches, the world locks up its spoons and packs off its womankind.

George Bernard Shaw

796 The food there is so bad there really ought to be a government health warning on the menu.

797 The art of medicine consists of amusing the patient while nature cures the disease.

Voltaire

798 I was asked to come six months ago. I did . . . but there was nobody here.

799   Oh, what a tangled web we weave
When first we practice to conceive.

Don Herold

800   A man taking over a responsible job was handed two
envelopes by his predecessor and told only to open them
if things became really rough. The first time he was in
despair he opened an envelope and the message inside
read 'Blame me.' When some months later he was forced
to open the second envelope it read 'Prepare two
envelopes.'

801   She got her good looks from her father—he's a
plastic surgeon.

Groucho Marx

802   As a golfer he's spent so long in bunkers he gets fan
mail from Rommel.

803   Laugh and the world laughs with you; be prompt
and you dine alone.

Gerald Barzan

804   She was the Avon rep . . . in Holloway.

805   (If a dinner is running very late)
'Good morning.'

806   Newspaper editors are men who separate the wheat
from the chaff, and then print the chaff.

Adlai Stevenson

807   X (someone in the news for bad behaviour) has also
sent his apologies . . . in case he comes later.

808   His parents couldn't even afford laxatives when he
was a child. They used to sit him on the potty and tell him
ghost stories.

809   Freedom of the press is limited to those who
own one.

A. J. Liebling

810   There's an old Croatian proverb . . . which you may
have forgotten.

811   When I was young I thought that money was the most important thing in life; now that I am old I know that it is.

Oscar Wilde

812   His trainer believes that sex does not impair his sporting performance . . . and he's just run the 100 yards in 3½ minutes.

813   If he really thinks there is no distinction between vice and virtue, when he leaves our house let us count our spoons.

Samuel Johnson

814   The town is beautifully laid out. Mind, I'm not sure when it died.

815   If someone says it's not the money, it's the principle . . . it's the money.

816   Growing old isn't so bad when you consider the alternative.

Maurice Chevalier

817   He's so desperate for female company that he gatecrashes Tupperware parties.

818   He is totally unspoilt by . . . failure.

819   He knows nothing and he thinks he knows everything. That points clearly to a political career.

George Bernard Shaw

820   I liked the meal . . . I'm trying to give up rich food.

821   I occasionally play works by comtemporary composers for two reasons. First to discourage the composer from writing any more and secondly to remind myself how much I appreciate Beethoven.

Jascha Heifetz

822   I've had a wonderful evening . . . but this wasn't it.

823   Interesting to have the soup and the wine served at the same temperature.

824   That all-softening, over-powering knell,
    The tocsin of the soul—the dinner bell.

Lord Byron

825   His wife's credit card had been stolen but he's not reported it because the thief is spending less than she did.

826   Wagner's music is better than it sounds.

Mark Twain

827   They call her 'wee' because she keeps saying yes to Frenchmen.

828   I can enjoy flowers quite happily without translating them into Latin.

Cornelia Otis Skinner

829   (If running late)
The date on my watch has never changed during a dinner before.

830   It's not true that he finds *Coronation Street* an intellectual challenge.

831   He's on a high-fibre diet—chipboard from DIY shops.

832   I got the bill for my surgery. Now I know what those doctors were wearing masks for.

James H. Boren

833   You've had turkey stuffed with sage. Now you've got a sage stuffed with turkey.

834   Never vote for the best candidate, vote for the one who will do the least harm.

Frank Dane

835   Don't applaud yet . . . I've got a lousy finish.

836   He's going to saw a woman in half . . . lengthways.

837   He uses statistics as a drunken man uses lamp-posts—for support rather than for illumination.

Andrew Lang

838   Since he started to wear a pace-maker, every time he makes love his garage door opens.

839   A director must be a policeman, a midwife, a psychoanalyst, a sycophant and a bastard.

Billy Wilder

840   I've known your chairman for . . . half an hour.

841   He's gone to that great resting place . . . he's got a job at (store or garage to be ribbed).

842   If all economists were laid end to end, they would not reach a conclusion.

George Bernard Shaw

843   I feel rather like the planning officer who put prunes on his pizza . . . I am deeply moved.

844   He drank so much that when we came back through customs we had to pay duty on him.

845   A government that robs Peter to pay Paul can always depend upon the support of Paul.

George Bernard Shaw

846   A harridan staggered into a bar with a parrot on her shoulder and shouted 'Whoever can guess the weight of this bird can spend the night with me free.'
Wag: '3½ tons.'
Woman: 'That's near enough.'

847   I was late because I followed a (profession to rib) at confession. I had to wait nearly three hours.

848   It is difficult to get a man to understand something when his salary depends upon his not understanding it.

Upton Sinclair

849   Giving prizes away at a girls' school and trying to show an interest, I whispered to one 18 year old: 'What are you planning to do when you leave here?' She whispered back that she had been thinking of going straight home.

850   You can get an Action Man doll of a stockbroker. Show it a press clip of a recession and it wets itself.

851   If you watch a game, it's fun. If you play, it's recreation. If you work at it, it's golf.

Bob Hope

852   I notice that the waiters here wear gloves. I wonder what they're afraid of catching?

853   The cost of living has gone up another dollar a quart.

W. C. Fields

854   So when the chairman offered to go halves with the cost of my meal, of course I accepted.

855   Can you hear at the back? No? Then how do you know what I said?

856   He has been suffering from love bites . . . mainly self-inflicted.

857   Never put off till tomorrow what you can do the day after tomorrow.

Mark Twain

858   If you stop your car and shout 'Which way?' 90 per cent will say 'Straight on'.

859   (About a company 'system'.)
It is really the bureaucratic equivalent of breaking wind.

860   Early to bed and early to rise is a bad rule for anyone who wishes to become acquainted with our most prominent and influential people.

George Ade

861   The Welsh keep a welcome in the valleys . . . but just try getting invited into their homes.

862   I was told to watch the British Lions . . . so I went to Longleat.

863   Many a good story has been ruined by over-verification.

864   Architects cover their mistakes with ivy, brides with maonnaise, doctors with sods.

865   When I was a kid I said to my father one afternoon, 'Daddy, will you take me to the zoo?' He answered, 'If the zoo wants you let them come and get you.'

866   She wears black garters in memory of those who've passed beyond.

867 I kissed my first woman and smoked my first cigarette on the same day. I have never had time for tobacco since.

Arturo Toscanini

868 He is such a dedicated exhibitionist that when it's very cold he jumps out in front of girls and describes himself.

869 He was in, but his answering machine was abroad.

870 I'm a practising heterosexual . . . but bisexuality immediately doubles your chances for a date on Saturday night.

Woody Allen

871 As I'd boasted I liked kids, my neighbour chided me when I complained bitterly that his nine-year-old had walked on my new drive before it was set. I explained that I liked kids in the abstract . . . not in the concrete.

872 There were tears in his eyes . . . it could have been the wine of course.

873 In the future, cars may even be powered by body heat, with pictures of nudes flashed on the windscreen to increase speed. Mind, with my sex drive I'd probably go into reverse.

874 City types just seem to go into wine bars . . . and whine.

875 He ran a raffle for a pedigree dog and sold 5,000 tickets at £1 each. Sadly the dog died on the way to the winner. Mind, he was very fair about it—he gave the bloke his £1 back.

876 There's such an urge to condense things for the TV news that if Moses arrived with the Ten Commandments today, he'd be asked to tell us about the most important three.

877 Writing is the only profession where no-one considers you ridiculous if you earn no money.

Jules Renard

878   You're obviously my kind of audience . . . I can smell the brown ale and crisps.

879   I know you're not professional (estate agents). You make an honest living.

880   (At a retirement presentation)
I'm sorry Fred, but X (accountant) wants you to stay for another seven weeks—he's found another box of your headed notepaper which needs using up.

881   I had hoped to bring you an aerial shot of (town or factory) but unfortunately somebody moved.

882   When she gets obscene phone calls, they reverse the charges.

883   He looked pale so I thrust his head firmly between his legs. It was a pity he was smoking at the time.

884   When you've made love to a Russian girl, she will say, 'You have possessed my body, but you will never possess my mind.' An American girl will say, 'What did you say your name is?' An English girl will say, 'Do you feel better now, love?'

885   If you want to get rich from writing, write the sort of thing that's read by persons who move their lips when they're reading to themselves.

Don Marquis

886   When you're up to your backside in alligators it's difficult to remember that the objective is to drain the swamp.

887   I had intended to talk about (controversial issue) but I hate to see grown men cry.

888   The Government are really worried about the number of old age pensioners in Britain. They don't understand how they can live so long under such awful conditions.

889   Lord give me chastity—but not yet.

St Augustine

890   Attractive girl to doctor: 'Where shall I put my clothes?'
Doctor: 'Over there . . . on top of mine.'

891 The more potent a man becomes in the bedroom, the more potent he is in business.

Dr David Reuben

892 I've been in better-looking jails.

893 He's so neurotic he has his annual check-up every month.

894 Cowardice increases in proportion to the amount of money invested.

895 The trouble with life is that there are so many beautiful women and so little time.

John Barrymore

896 (After a joke has flopped)
I'd commit suicide . . . but what could I do for an encore?

897 The personnel department not only knows where the bodies are buried . . . it knows who still has the shovel.

898 There he sits . . . with his hand where his heart used to be.

899 He's got a new job . . . as a bouncer at Mothercare.

900 When a man says he approves of something in principle, it means he hasn't the slightest intention of putting it into practice.

Prince Otto von Bismarck

901 It is said one should speak in public for the same length of time one can make love in private . . . this will not be a long speech.

902 There he sits . . . in his wig from Allied Carpets.

903 He used to be a piano player . . . in a marching band.

904 Religion is excellent stuff for keeping common people quiet.

Napoleon Bonaparte

905 He lead the Irish assault on Mount Everest . . . but they ran out of scaffolding.

906   I'm so unlucky I put a coin in a slot machine in Las Vegas . . . and three prunes came up.

907   I'm getting to the age when I prefer big numbers on calendars to nudes.

908   He shot a 68 . . . and tomorrow he's going to tackle the second hole.

909   I wouldn't say he drinks . . . but when I met him in Trafalgar Square he was throwing coins for the lions to fetch.

910   He got the lumps on his head trying to hang himself with a piece of elastic.

911   Following X (good speaker) makes me feel rather as if I am about to make love to (film or TV star in the news for loves/marriages). I feel it's been done before, and it's probably been done a great deal better.

912   He thought *coq au vin* was a bunk-up in the back of a Transit.

913   We found a cure for his car-sickness—we put a £5 note between his teeth.

914   I wouldn't say the band's bad, but that's the first time I've heard a drummer play the melody line.

915   I sense you've enjoyed the meal . . . you obviously like hospital food.

916   When your friends begin to flatter you on how young you look, it's a sure sign you're getting old.

Mark Twain

917   I would have liked to have joined the scouts, but my parents didn't want me to be linked to a paramilitary organization.

918   A consultant knows 832 ways of making love . . . but hasn't got a girlfriend.

919   When he arrived in heaven he was asked to be quiet and tiptoe past one room. When he asked why, St Peter said, 'That's reserved for members of (rival club or organization) . . . they think they're the only ones up here.'

920 His voice was trained . . . his parents used to put paper down on the floor.

921 We encountered a tribe of short-sighted Indians who couldn't tell heads from tails. They had an unusual collection of scalps.

922 The cricketer was faced with a paternity suit and asked what grounds. He was told Lords, the Oval, Trent Bridge . . . .

923 He became a father today. There'll be hell to pay if his wife finds out.

924 I'm not fit . . . I get winded playing Scrabble.

925 It's an expensive town. I built a sandcastle . . . and got a rates demand.

926 In sexual intercourse, it's quality not quantity that counts.

Dr David Reuben

927 He was so upset he was beside himself. And you never saw such an unattractive couple.

928 I even sent my details to the Lonely Hearts Club . . . but they wrote back to say there weren't *that* lonely.

929 He's so cautious he worries about whether it's safe to put his teeth in water when he's abroad.

930 He manages on the 'hook-and-eye' principle . . . 'who can I' pass the problem to?

931 I wouldn't say he drinks . . . but when I met him he was putting coins into a drain outside Big Ben, hoping to read his weight.

932 He got the Salesman of the Year award . . . for selling a double bed to the Pope.

933 The last toast-master I met introduced me by saying 'Pray for the silence of our distinguished guest.'

934 He has left off reading altogether to the great improvement of his originality.

Charles Lamb

935 It should have been an X-piece band . . . but the other two failed the dope test.

936 It should have been an X-piece band . . . but we couldn't get bail for the other two.

937 (About the band)
It was the best the Job Centre could do at short notice.

938 Paddy was told to impress girls on the beach he should slip a potato inside his trunks. After an unsuccessful holiday it was gently explained to him that he should have put it down the *front*.

939 I suspect I stand at the end of a long but distinguished line of refusals.

940 They say he's the Rolls-Royce of speakers . . . well-oiled, almost inaudible and goes for a long, long time.

941 He had the sort of face that always wants to see the manager.

942 He has become a professional model—they use his picture on poison bottles.

943 I've got to the age where I can't take 'yes' for an answer.

944 I hope they will be as happy as my wife and I thought we were going to be.

945 A pessimist is a man who thinks all women are bad. An optimist is one who hopes they are.

Chauncey Depew

946 (At scruffy venue)
How far off Broadway can you get?

947 He has written his autobiography: *How to Succeed in Business by Being Really Trying*.

948 And remember—when one door closes, another always slams in your face.

949 We had to have the dog put down for worrying sheep—it used to slink up to them and whisper, 'Mint sauce'.

950 Sometimes at functions you get poor food, indifferent company and so on . . . and tonight is no exception.

951 (If proposing a toast)
I've been asked to say something nice about X (the association). I don't see why I should . . . they've never said anything nice about me.

952 When a rugby player yelled as his dislocated shoulder received attention, the nurse pointed out that a woman had just given birth to a baby with far less fuss. 'Maybe', said the player, 'but let's see what happens if you try to put it back.'

953 He stood by my side when my house caught fire; he stood by my side when my car crashed (continue with series of sagas). Yes, he's a perfect b... jinx for me.

954 He has an Irish cat. It doesn't matter what height you drop it from . . . it lands on its head.

955 He's been reading (any appropriate book) . . . in the pop-up edition.

956 We used a model of him as a scarecrow—the birds brought back seed they'd pinched the previous year.

957 This place has a wonderful atmosphere . . . like a clinic.

958 It's a rough area. I put my hand out to signal I was turning . . . and had my watch pinched.

959 You have to admire politicians' tenacity. There's a policeman outside Number 10 right round the clock . . . but the Prime Minister still gets out.

960 One of his ancestors had a suspended sentence . . . they hung him.

961 He was rushed to hospital with a suspected hole-in-the-heart. It turned out to be a Polo mint in his pyjama pocket.

962 He's just finished his first novel. He's hoping to read another one soon.

963   He's never been businessman of the year. He was nominated by *Playboy* magazine for licentious executive of the month but, sadly, he failed the practical.

964   Men will follow him anywhere . . . out of curiosity.

965   I'm getting to the age when I feel my corns more than my oats.

966   I'm not a proud speaker. If you don't wish to applaud I'll settle for enthusiastic nods.

967   It's getting very difficult to forecast future market trends. As an example, the motor industry reckons that eight years ago every car had 2.8 passengers; three years ago every car had 1.7. This seems to indicate that in a few years' time every third car on the M1 will be empty.

968   He's so fat that when he takes a shower the water runs uphill.

969   In English hotels they get up at 5 a.m. to cook breakfast . . . then serve it when you come down at 9 a.m.

970   And now a word for any nymphomaniacs here tonight . . . hallo.

971   His car has a new unbreakable filler cap—a lump of rag.

972   We've enjoyed the food, Mr Chairman, and would ask you to convey our thanks to the temporary chef.

973   Your chairman said I would be addressing the cream of the profession. Looking at you I think he just meant that you are rising very slowly to the top.

974   This place is so elegant even the alphabet soup spells polite words.

975   A man complained to his doctor that the first time he made love to his new wife he was bitterly cold, the second time he was uncomfortably hot. The doctor could find nothing wrong with him and called the wife to investigate further. She laughed and explained that the first time had been in January . . . the second in August.

976 You can always tell an (Oxford/Harvard or whatever) man. Whether or not he will understand you is another matter.

977 Lloyds started in a coffee house . . . and has ended in a coffee percolator.

978 My local garage has a customer who has complained that the dipstick on his car isn't long enough to reach the oil.

979 This novel is not to be tossed lightly aside, but to be hurled with great force.

Dorothy Parker

980 An officer asked a lady of the night 'How much for the pleasure of my company?'
She replied: '£50, dearie.'
Officer: 'Fine. Company, by the left . . .'

981 Every other creature has the sense to lie down after a good meal.

982 (Following long speeches)
Good evening. Do I have time for more?

983 I hadn't spoken to him for two days . . . I didn't want to interrupt him.

984 He was voted the school dropout most likely to succeed.

985 She is working to put her son through . . . prison.

986 I had a good day in (dowdy town) yesterday—I wasn't mugged.

987 He's a religious fanatic . . . he beats up nuns.

988 The way you lot trade makes the Mafia look effeminate.

989 I keep his/her picture over the mantlepiece at home. It keeps the kids away from the fire.

990 If you're not in bed here by 10.30 p.m. the bed-bugs come down looking for you.

991   After 18 years they finally achieved sexual compata-
bility last night—they both had headaches.

992   (About a profession)
Well, I suppose it's inside work and no heavy lifting.

993   A speech is a solemn responsibility. The man who
makes a bad 30-minute speech to 200 people wastes only a
half-hour of his own time. But he wastes 100 hours of the
audience's time—more than four days—which should be a
hanging offence.

Jenkin Lloyd Jones

994   If you steal from one another it's plagiarism; if you
steal from many, it's research.

Wilson Mizner

995   Originality is the art of concealing your source.

Franklin P. Jones

Hecklers

996   Careful, you're getting over-excited. There'll be tears
before bedtime.

997   Would you move that man closer to the wall, please?
That's plastered, too.

998   You must be a bundle of fun at home.

999   Were you there for the fitting of that suit?

1000   You seem happy tonight. No school tomorrow?

1001   Would you mind standing up? I know what you
are, I just wanted to see what one looks like.

1002   Please pour that man back into the bottle.

1003   It just shows the effect of drinking on an empty
head.

1004   There's conclusive proof that brain transplants
don't work.

1005 I seem to recall you were in here when I spoke ten years ago. I remember that suit.

1006 One fool at a time please.

1007 If I want you, I'll rattle your cage.

1008 Is that your own mouth, or are you breaking it in for an idiot?

1009 Your mind should be open—not your mouth.

1010 Every minute a poet is born.

1011 I see they've named a town after you, sir. Leatherhead.

Index of quotations

5000 ONE AND TWO LINERS FOR ANY AND EVERY OCCASION

Leo

A wo... ...ect.
Here... ...een
spec... ...or's
colle... ...ith
pun... ...ble
for ... ...ed
any... ...do
bett... ...ou
can ... ...our
quic... ...can
look... ...lar
topi... ...nce
guid... ... of
addi...